Advanced Business Analytics

Saumitra N. Bhaduri · David Fogarty

Advanced Business Analytics

Essentials for Developing a Competitive Advantage

Springer

Saumitra N. Bhaduri
Madras School of Economics
Chennai, Tamil Nadu
India

David Fogarty
University of Liverpool
Merseyside, Liverpool
UK

ISBN 978-981-10-0726-2 ISBN 978-981-10-0727-9 (eBook)
DOI 10.1007/978-981-10-0727-9

Library of Congress Control Number: 2016938666

Printed on acid-free paper

This Springer imprint is published by Springer Nature
The registered company is Springer Science+Business Media Singapore Pte Ltd.

Contents

Authors and Contributors

About the Authors

Saumitra N. Bhaduri received his Master's degree in Econometric from Calcutta University, Kolkata, India, and his Ph.D. in Financial Economics from Indira Gandhi Institute of Development Research (IGIDR), Mumbai, India. He currently works as a professor at Madras School of Economics, Chennai, India, where he regularly offers courses on Financial Economics and Econometrics, and on Advanced Quantitative Techniques. In terms of his former career he also worked at GE Capital, the financial services division of the General Electric Company, and has held various quantitative analysis roles in the company's finance services. He also founded and headed the GE–MSE Decision Sciences Laboratory where he was responsible for developing state-of-the-art research output for GE. He has also published several research articles in various international journals. His research interests include: Financial Economics and Econometrics, Quantitative Techniques and Advanced Analytics.

David Fogarty received his B.S. in International Relations from Connecticut State University, USA, his Ph.D. in Applied Statistics from Leeds Metropolitan University, UK, and his MBA with a concentration in International Business from Fairfield University, USA. He also has a post-graduate qualification from Columbia University in NYC. In terms of his professional career, he currently works at a Fortune 100 health insurance company as the Chief Analytics Officer or Head of Global Customer Value Management and Growth Analytics. In terms of his former career, Dr. Fogarty also worked for 20 years at GE Capital, the financial services division of the General Electric Company, and has held various quantitative analysis roles across several functions, including risk management and marketing, both internationally and in the US. He currently holds over 10 US patents or patents pending on business analytics algorithms.

In addition to his work as a practitioner Dr. Fogarty has over 10 years of teaching experience and has held various adjunct academic appointments at both the graduate and undergraduate level in statistics, international management and quantitative analysis at the University of Liverpool (UK), Trident University (USA), Manhattanville College (USA), University of New Haven (USA), SUNY Purchase College (USA), Manhattan College (USA), LIM College (USA), the University of Phoenix (USA), Chancellor University (USA), Alliant University International (USA) and the Jack Welch management Institute at Strayer University (USA). Dr. Fogarty is also an "Honorary Professor" at the Madras School of Economics in Chennai, India and has given guest lectures in Asia at East China Normal University (Shanghai, China), Ivey Business School (Hong Kong, China), and the City University of Hong Kong. He has also taught business analytics courses at the esteemed GE Crotonville Management Development Institute in Crotonville, New York. Since obtaining his Ph.D., he has continued to collaborate with several universities and leading academics to pursue academic research and has several published research papers in peer-reviewed academic journals. His research interests include: how to conduct analysis with missing data, the cultural meaning of data, integrating genetic algorithms into the statistical science framework, and many other topics related to quantitative analysis in business.

Contributors

S. Raja Sethu Durai Madras School of Economics, Chennai, India

V. Anuradha Madras School of Economics, Chennai, India

Avanti George Madras School of Economics, Chennai, India

List of Figures

List of Tables

Chapter 1
Introduction and Overview

David Fogarty

Analytics for business as we know it in terms of predictive analytics probably started in ancient Roman times when the concept of insurance was first created. The Romans were particularly concerned with the rituals around death and dying and therefore first created the concept of funeral insurance. Today, the selling of funeral insurance through direct TV is often viewed by the regulators and the public alike as a deceptive substitute for life insurance targeted to low fixed-income elderly folks. Little do they realize that the product has been around for literally thousands of years! This process of diversifying risk through insurance gradually advanced until the concepts of life tables were introduced by Edmund Halley of Halley's comet fame in 1693. Halley's work followed that of John Graunt, a London draper who in 1662 discovered that patterns of longevity and death in a defined group, or cohort followed predictable patterns. This was the case despite the uncertainty about the future longevity or mortality of any one individual person. Life tables made it possible to set up an insurance product or policy in order to be able to provide life insurance or pensions for a group of people, and to calculate with some degree of accuracy, how much each person in the group should contribute to a common fund assumed to earn a fixed rate of interest. Halley both constructed his own life table in addition to demonstrating a method of using it in order to calculate a premium from his life table. A premium refers to the amount of money someone of a given age (or other attributes) should pay to purchase a life annuity.

While the previous examples have shown that analytics for business has been around for some time, it is only relatively recently that there has been an increased emphasis on the use of analytics in the modern business scenario.

A couple of decades ago, even in a major Fortune 200 company, surprisingly, there was very little use of data to make decisions. Most managers really did not use computers or numbers of any kind to manage their businesses. They managed literally by walking the aisles and by "the seat of their pants." Companies which had data in digital format and had the need to conduct analytics were the early movers in this area. Credit card companies with their need for credit scoring and catalogue/direct marketing companies with their need to target customer lists are

S.N. Bhaduri and D. Fogarty, *Advanced Business Analytics*,
DOI 10.1007/978-981-10-0727-9_1

two examples of these. The transition over the past several decades to an absolute demand for managing by the numbers is both the result of technology advances and a generational shift in the business world as generation x and y managers arrive with computer training and familiarity with more advanced quantitative methods which can be executed with the aid of technology.

Analytics are gaining increasing importance in the global marketplace both as a basis for competition and being able to add shareholder value through improving core growth and productivity. Much of this can be attributed to the expansion of e-commerce and the advent of high-speed computers and technology. Data capture technology today is advancing faster than data technology. Moreover, in the field of predictive analytics including propensity and profitability modeling, improvements are possible through being able to better explore growing data sources like the Web, electronic payment systems, and swelling corporate data warehouses. From the perspective of firsthand experience, we can conclude that hiring skilled people to do this kind of work in Asia is a blood sport! As these sources of data continue to grow, companies are facing stiff competition in the global labor markets for highly skilled employees who can analyze and extract value from the data. The distinguished statistician Bradley Efron (2008) commented how technology is destiny in science and statisticians are adapting to modern technology which permits a 1000-fold increase in information collection. Moreover, in his 2004 presidential address at the Joint Statistical Meetings which is a gathering of the world's top statisticians from several statistical societies, Efron made the following points: "Now the planets may be aligning for statistics. New technology, electronic computation, has broken the bottleneck of calculation that limited classical statistical theory. At the same time, an onrush of important new questions has come upon us, in the form of huge data sets and large-scale inference problems. I believe that the statisticians of this generation will participate in a new age of statistical innovation that may trivialize the golden age of Fisher, Neyman, Hotelling, and Wald."

Evolving corporate data warehouses over the last 20 years coupled with competitive pressures and new generations of management armed with quantitative and computing skills have also been responsible for the growth in the need for advanced analytics. Kimball (2002) analyzed the evolution of data warehouses in the 1980s and 1990s and reported that each had their distinctive "marquee" applications. For instance, in the early 1980s, a 50-MB database was considered pretty large. But, firms in this era were content to be able to analyze the basic sales numbers of an organization. The marquee data warehousing application of the 1980s was shipments and market share in that managers at the time were delighted to see how much product we shipped from month to month and in some cases what fraction of the total market that represented. Kimball (2002) also noted that these early data warehousing applications represented the first time firms could drill down from the annual report to start analyzing the components of their businesses. In the 1980s, with the exception of a few key industries, the analytics that firms used were very simple: this month versus last month or this month versus a year ago. And perhaps the most challenging calculation for early data miners was the share of a market this month versus the same share a year ago.

By the early 1990s, Kimball (2002) noted that our capacities, techniques, and analytic expectations had progressed beyond simple shipments and share numbers to demand a full analysis of profitability at an individual customer level. At the beginning of the 1990s, the most sophisticated data warehouses were already analyzing revenue at the individual store or branch level. Certainly by the end of the 1990s, we were able to capture and store the most atomic transactions of our businesses in the data warehouse. The marquee data warehouse application of the 1990s was customer profitability. Firms developed techniques for tying together the disparate revenue and cost data sources in order to assemble a complete view of profitability. Firms like Royal Bank of Canada (RBC) developed some notable core competence in this area. The extreme atomic detail of the data allowed us to tag each transaction with the exact product and customer. In this way, firms could roll up a full P&L perspective for each customer and product line (Kimball 2002).

Although the quantity of data available for analysis increased by at least a factor of 1,000 between the 1980s and 1990s, there was no measurable increase in the sophistication of analytic techniques which were deployed on the data. Most firms had their hands full just wrangling the huge databases. While there was some modest increase in the use of data mining techniques, these advanced analytic approaches remained a tiny fraction of the data warehouse activities in firms. However, there was a significant improvement in the ease of use of end-user tools for querying and reporting. The explicit SQL user interfaces of the 1980s mercifully gave way in the 1990s to much more powerful user interfaces for combining data from multiple sources, highlighting exceptions, and pivoting the data at the user's desktop to make the numbers pop.

The long cycle time leading to the adoption of advanced analytic techniques in the 1990s was most likely due to cultural resistance on behalf of managers within the firms. Business management has always been reluctant to trust something it does not really understand. The combination of statistics and technology working together was beyond the training and experience of most managers in firms over the past two decades.

At the end of the 1990s, CRM emerged as an important new data warehousing application. CRM extended the notion of customer profitability to include understanding the complete customer relationship. But CRM as implemented in the 1990s was still just a transactional perspective on the customer. Firms counted the number of times the customer visited their stores or Web sites. For example, they would measure customer satisfaction by the ratio of successful product deliveries to the total or by the change in the number of complaints. The sophistication of the analytic techniques was reminiscent of the kinds of counts and comparisons which were used by firms for shipments and share calculations in the early 1980s. The problem with this view of customer profitability is that it was working backward from the present and was not in any way predictive of what could occur in the future.

But marketing managers are constantly looking for new competitive angles. Today's marketing managers have a distinctly different challenge. Seybor (2007) asserts that while marketing used to be described as more of an art than a science, the explosion of Web technology and analytical tools demands that marketers 124 literally put down their crayons and begin to use calculators for getting their work done. Marketing's key role is to develop a relationship with the customers which today are more often accessible electronically. Marketing managers will get the next competitive edge when they can understand, predict, and influence individual customer behavior.

At the same time, the sources of data have descended to the subtransactional level. It seemed in the late 1990s that by capturing every atomic sales transaction, we could somehow arrive at a fundamental foundation for all possible data. But the development of CRM and the capture of presales customer behavior have opened up potentially another factor of 1,000 in the amount of data a firm can collect about its customers. These new data sources include individual page requests tracking visitors on the Web, call center logs relating to product information and customer support, market basket information from retail and financial companies, and promotion response tracking. For instance, at a home improvement store analysts can track a customer's transaction down to what brand of portable drill they are buying. We are just in the dawn of experiencing explosive growth of these subtransactional data sources. Soon, we will all have global positioning systems embedded not only in our cars, but also in our passports and our credit cards. At the same time, our increased security needs will allow us to see customers coming and going from many of our stores and offices. This type of technology is already being deployed to fight crime and prevent terrorist acts. Of course privacy concerns will legitimately slow down and regulate the growth of using the data from these technologies (Kimball 2002); however, in a marketplace where the call for accountability and return on investment seems to drown out other marketing goals, strategic database marketing services that include advanced analytics are in more demand and more powerful than ever (Krol 2006).

The analysis of actual (not surveyed) customer behavior will be the preeminent data warehousing application in the 2000s. Surveys which are used by traditional market research companies tell firms what customers intend to do or say that they do. Analysis of customer behavior actually tells firms what customers are really doing. There is a marked difference between these two. For instance, a survey of customers of a credit card company will reveal that almost all prefer a low rate of interest on their financial services product. However, when you examine the actual behavior of these same customers that expressed the desire to have a low rate of interest, some will actually be heavy users of the product at higher rates of interest than their previous response indicated. The reason behind this is that people often behave differently than they respond to questions in a survey. This bias is responsible for billions in opportunity costs for firms who rely heavily on market research for insights and is stimulating the growth of data warehousing, an advanced analytics. Therefore, firms will continue to expand their analyses of both individual and commercial customer behaviors.

Due to recent advances in high-speed computing technology, sophisticated algorithms for prediction have been introduced. Bauer (2006) developed a useful framework for model types and the advanced algorithms which support these. The framework insures that the firm or organization analysis needs to drive the solution methodology rather than the choice of algorithms dictating the analysis options. This avoids what he referred to as “algorithm nirvana” where a myriad of analysis options can lead to analysis–paralysis syndrome.

Genetic algorithms are an example of the sophisticated algorithms which have been developed. Genetic algorithms were actually originally introduced decades ago by John Holland but were not viable due to the lack of available computing technology (Bhaskar et al. 2007). This method which focuses largely on the nature of volatility stretches the limits of even the most high-powered computers. Genetic algorithms operate with the objective of replicating the manner in which genes are passed from one generation to the next. The surviving genes create models that form the most durable and effective offspring (Bernstein 1998).

While there are many inherent risks and assumptions in using genetic algorithms, there are also some definite advantages. The first advantage includes its ability to mitigate some of the negative effects of Simpson’s paradox and corollary’s which state that an association between two variables can be reversed upon introduction of a third variable. In addition, variables that by themselves may seem insignificant but when included with others can become important (multivariate and interaction). Finally, variables that by themselves may seem significant but when included with others can become irrelevant. Therefore, given Simpson’s paradox and corollary’s suboptimal models are yielded when data reduction is performed early in the model building process and analysis is restricted to first-order correlation. However, the vast majority of credit scoring techniques requires and recommends data reduction prior to model building and render primarily univariate consideration. Moreover, modeling in complex systems requires the simultaneous optimization of variable selection, coefficient setting, missing data management, interaction detection, and variable transformation. Searching for optimal solution through all possible variable combinations is impractical. For example, selecting just 10 in 25 variables equals 11 trillion combinations of variables. There are even more possibilities when transformations or interactions are included.

Therefore, the genetic algorithms enable some key improvements for model development. One benefit is significantly reduced model development time by 50–74 % through advanced data preparation processing. Also, genetic algorithms allow the realization of increased model “lift” typically ranging from 5 to 15 % over traditional approaches such as logistic regression. Another benefit of genetic algorithms is that they provide an audit function where all models developed in an organization by trained statisticians can be monitored by the GAs for quality assurance. Finally, genetic algorithms for model development enable improvements in model R&D and hypothesis testing by allowing the exploration of 100 % of the data attributes and develop new insights by exploring more data and uncovering new market opportunities. At GE, genetic algorithms have been utilized broadly across its diverse business lines anywhere from optimizing power plants in the GE Energy business to predict failures of industrial equipment in the GE Industrial business to develop consumer credit scores used in GE Money businesses across the globe (Bhaskar et al. 2007).

Other advanced techniques include artificial neural networks. Artificial neural networks are defined as computational machines designed to model the way in which the human brain performs a particular task or function of interest. Artificial neural network classifiers have received a great deal of attention in the last several decades primarily for their capabilities of automation, robustness to outliers in the data, and their ability to classify based on nonlinear patterns in the data. Moreover, these tools have had a tremendous impact on firms when searching for information to solve problems that human analyses could not find. For instance, artificial neural networks have been used very successfully in commercial applications to detect fraudulent customers applying for consumer credit as they are able to use their nonlinear processing capabilities to detect inconsistencies in the application process (Fogarty 2001).

All of these new advanced algorithms used to analyze the data must be fulfilled by advanced processing capabilities enabled by IT departments. Monash (2005) pointed out that although Moore's law has been going strong for decades, the processing power needed to do advanced analytics may actually exceed the speed at which this has been evolving.

This adaptation is often in the form of advanced algorithms enabling the extract of critical insights from this vast amount of stored data. Areas which have traditionally been stored via physical files are now increasingly being stored electronically. Medical records are one such example which are coming under increasing pressure to be recorded electronically. Proof of this has been documented in the popular book on analytics by Davenport and Harris called "Competing on Analytics" where the main premise found through extensive research is that some companies take analytics to the next level by not only using it to add value within the firm but also using it as a basis for competing. In their book, Davenport and Harris outline five factors that distinguish analytic competitors from their counterparts. The first is on the data side, and all analytic competitors have clean data easily accessible in a data warehouse. Moreover, analytical competitors take it one step further and even create their own new data types. For instance, the Boston Red Sox created their run production metrics. Progressive insurance installs a probe in its customer's cars to collect additional data and Gallo Winery created a whole series of metrics on growing grapes and creating wines. Finally, GE Money, the largest global retail finance provider in the world, used their global scale and data to create unique analytic products that combine customer data from the retail credit portfolio and retail transaction data to provide unique insights into how customers behave, which goes several steps beyond what traditional marketing research can do. The second factor is enterprise where analytic competitors have a centralized analytics team or thought leadership instead of fragmented silos within the organization. Fragmented analytic silos without a common strategy for analytics will not enable information technology teams to organize the data in a cohesive strategy resulting in further challenges within the organization in terms of making better decisions with the data. The third is leadership where leaders from the top down are driving the process of using analytics as a basis for competition with passion and commitment. The fourth factor is people. Analytic competitors have an organization with a predictable amount of analytic experts, semiprofessionals, and analytical amateurs. The fifth factor is targets. At first, analytic competitors pick a few core competencies and then target very deep into those competencies. After they achieve the required depth, they go very broad. Walmart, for example, has targeted very deep into the supply chain area and is now extending this competency to other areas. In addition to the book, Davenport and Harris wrote a summary article on the topic in the Harvard Business Review and had the most downloaded article ever in the journal's history. Finally, there have been several recent articles in popular business media including the BusinessWeek article "Math will Rock Your World" and the Economist article "Using Algorithms in business." Other popular books recently published include "Super Crunchers" by Ian Ayres.

The growth of SAS Institute as statistical software and services company into the largest privately held software company in the world with nearly $2 billion annual revenues, 10,000 employees, and over 400 offices worldwide (Datamonitor 2007) is another testament to the incredible growth and importance of analytics in the world today. Also, specialty analytic consulting firms such as Fair Isaac spend over 10 % of their annual revenues on research and development for advanced analytics. Even large traditional computer companies like IBM are now getting in the game through their acquisitions of companies such as I-Log and SPSS.

Educational institutions like the Indian Institute of Management in Ahmedabad have sponsored educational programs for enabling managers to make better decisions in their firms. More recently, this idea has even gathered more momentum in that the Madras School of Economics and the North Carolina State University have now started thinking about offering specialized degree programs in advanced analytics which serve as feeders for businesses like GE and Capital One to provide analysts to solve tough business problems using advanced analytic algorithms. As advanced analytics gains popularity and we enter a new data-driven era, not only firms must put these practices into place at a high level, but also they must find armies of workers to support the change. As the demand for employees with an advanced understanding of analytical technologies increases, the pool of knowledge workers steadily diminishes. Universities across the globe are beginning to wake up and address this demand for knowledge workers in advanced analytics.

Professional sports are another area which has greatly benefited from the use of advanced analytics. Besides the groundbreaking work done by the Oakland A's, Boston Red Sox, and New England Patriots as mentioned by Davenport and Harris and in the book Moneyball by Michael Lewis, a top agent named Scott D. Boras pioneered the use of game statistics to help his clients train and perform better. This has helped him negotiate $3 billion in player contracts over the past 30 years, including $252 million over 10 years for Alex Rodriguez, the largest deal ever. As such, he is regarded as a trendsetter. What differentiates Boras from his peers and lends him his power is how he uses stats. Baseball is a game of history and numbers. Boras' approach has been to identify and organize data—stats—in a way that can explain his players' performance or help them study their success and failures on the field (Cole 2007).

In the early 1990s, Boras brought in a NASA computer scientist and a Harvard economics major to put together a database with stats from 1871 to the present day. The system, which costs millions of dollars to build, keeps score of every pitch and at bat in the major leagues in real time. The Boras Corp. headquarters in Newport Beach, Calif., resembles a Wall Street trading firm: rows and rows of desks filled with flat-screen panels displaying tickers of up-to-the-minute data of their client's performance (Cole 2007).

Advanced analytics has also caught up with the visual and speech recognition industry. For instance, with the latest evolution in surveillance monitoring advanced analytics serve as a critical component of a security operation. Without this capability, companies lack the ability to effectively monitor video from security cameras on a 24/7 basis. Advanced analytics apply behavioral recognition technology to identity potential security violations, such as an individual loitering in an unmanned pedestrian area late at night (Analyze This 2006). Firms that record voice conversations, most notably contact centers, are turning to advanced speech-enabled data mining to deliver more comprehensive analytics to improve performance, to help reduce the costs of operating the centers, and, in some cases, to help transition call centers from cost centers to profit centers through service to sales initiatives such as cross-sell and up-sell (Britt 2007).

In the world of e-business, advanced analytics is critical to effective business growth. Reimers (2000) discusses the various CRM tools in the marketplace used to personalize relationships on the Web and concludes that advanced technologies used for personalization including data mining, collaborative filtering, artificial intelligence, and neural networks can help make the online buying experience easier and more intuitive for customers and let E-businesses find ways to attract and retain valuable buyers.

Manufacturing is also benefiting from the use of advanced analytic algorithms in a diverse number of areas ranging from the manufacturing of semiconductor chips to statistical process control and the automated interpretation of control charts (Chen and Yeh 2004; Monch et al. 2006). In addition, genetic programming which is related to the genetic algorithm researchers has also been modeling the behavior of ants and these are being used to solve such tasks as defining a path for robotic applications (Oplatkova and Zelinka 2006).

Many ideas for new algorithms come from nature itself which usually has the most efficient way of conducting its business. For example, genetic algorithms mentioned above tap into to the laws of nature to efficiently find relationships in a very large search space. Moving to the very bottom of the food chain, researchers are finding that common slime molds found on the floors of temperate forests can have their behavior be modeled to find the best transportation routes in cities. Moving up the food chain researchers is modeling the behavior of ants in their colonies to find ever new ways to create efficient algorithms to find relationships in data. For example, ant behavior has been used to search a database and find the most robust segmentation models.

In addition to manufacturing, biological sciences including medicine have also benefited from advanced algorithms. For example, Tucker et al. (2006) have developed new temporal Bayesian classifiers for modeling muscular dystrophy expression data. In addition, advanced algorithms are being utilized to understand the association between genes and evasive diseases (McMillan McMillan et al. 2006). Also, explosive growth in the capture of medical data through advanced imaging technologies has driven the growth in using advanced algorithms to aid in the classification of patterns in these data (Pham et al. 2006). Finally, advanced algorithms to aid in decision making are being deployed in order to improve medical research across a variety of settings (Drummond and Sculpher 2006). All applications of these advanced algorithms will help medical professionals discover cures for diseases which have escaped previous medical research for decades.

As public utilities have become less regulated, they are also becoming more reliant on advanced analytics. For example, Arizona Public Service, which is the largest integrated electric utility in Arizona, with a diversified and growing energy portfolio that includes nearly 7500 MW of generation uses advanced algorithms to provide optimum power generation portfolio and ancillary services under complex fuel constraints (Tani 2007).

Gaming companies like Harrah's have always known since the 1950s that there is a strong Pareto principle happening with their gambling customers in that the top customers spend a disproportionate amount in the casinos as the lesser customers. In the 1950s, Bill Harrah use to personally call upon his top customers and give them special gifts such as antique roulette wheels. Today, with high-speed computers and data warehouses, gaming companies like Harrah's have turned this into a science offering platinum customers a ride to the casinos in private jets.

Companies operating in the same space compete on analytics in a different way. For instance, Capital One, a financial services company, developed almost entirely from organic growth competes on analytics. GE Money, a similar financial services company with a large credit card portfolio which developed primarily on the principle of acquisitions, competes on analytics on a different level. GE Money either acquires new businesses or engages in joint ventures on the basis of the acquired company or partner not having an analytic process embedded within their own business processes. Then through the process of information transfer through personnel in the form of STIRS or short-term international rotations coupled with providing its partners with access to its offshore intelligent factories which have over 600 Ph.D. Quantitative analysts create versions of Capital One in 54 different countries!

One may ask how does this fit into the context of parsimony? While parsimony is important at the individual model level when comparing different models produced from the same technique, this does not apply to the concept of advanced analytics where we are trying to use more advanced statistical techniques to extract greater information form the data. Also, parsimony is important when trying to sell an analytic concept which requires investment into the senior management team of a firm for the first time. However, once analytics imbedded into the process and the low-hanging fruits derived from using analytics have been extracted, more advanced modeling is necessary to keep generating increased benefits out of the process.

An example of this is at GE Capital where they initially acquired a consumer finance portfolio in Japan that had no analytics being used. They began the process by starting to use risk scorecards.

But over time, they advanced the analytics to the extent that they included all of the key factors related to consumer finance profitability eventually leading to full optimization. Many managers will claim that the easiest approach is better. While this may be true to a certain extent since analytics is difficult to explain to upper management, some of whom may have never been exposed to statistics. However, as more and more companies compete on analytics, the ability to launch an "arms race" based on advanced analytics will become even more important. An example of this is already happening in the insurance and credit card industries.

Capital One's entire business model is based on the fact that they have better models than their competitors. For instance, for statistical scorecard development, they will often try advanced techniques such as genetic algorithms or brain trees to see whether they are able to get in incremental lift in being able to predict the outcome. With these better models, they are gaining a competitive advantage over their competitors. With these better algorithms, not only are they able to attract better customers but also they are able to leave all the bad customers with their less analytically sophisticated competitors forcing a change in their portfolio mix.

Capital One finds the best statisticians from academia and consulting that have thought leadership in terms of academic research in certain areas and hire them into their internal environment. The internal environment looks more like a laboratory with stainless steel desks and exposed pipes than a traditional bank with mahogany desks as a testament to the corporate culture.

At GE Capital, they take a similar approach but in typical GE fashion turn it into a large-scale global process by utilizing their research laboratories including GE vaunted Global Research organization based in Schenectady New York and University labs at Madras School of Economic in Chennai, India, Central European University in Budapest, Hungary, and University of Connecticut in Stamford, Connecticut to develop the most advanced algorithms to better understand their customers. GE Capital has thousands of advanced analytic algorithms in use in its 54 businesses, and a substantial amount of decisions are made through the use of these models as they determine the future profitability of the customers within the firm.

Advanced analytics are transforming every aspect of the insurance value chain. The insurance industry has a significant amount of data at its disposal. Furthermore, except for traditional actuarial analyses handled primarily through the finance function, the majority of the information available from these data remains untapped.

The proliferation of data warehouses now being populated by insurance carriers is being utilized in the industry to begin using this information to improve processes and increase performance. By using advanced analytics and incorporating them into the claims process, insurance carriers can gain a competitive edge, increased productivity, and are able to significantly improve bottom-line results (Cacchione 2006; Coyne 2007).

Progressive insurance is a leader in the use of data to improve the insurance business. Progressive was the first insurance firm to discover that credit score was a reliable predictor of risk among drivers. They then used credit score to group customers based on risk and automated pricing to offer lower-risk customers best rates and risky driver high rates. They even have taken the bold move of offering the competitors quotes on their Web sites. Management at Progressive are so confident in their ability to use analytics to price a policy that if a competitor has a significantly lower price, then Progressive will even raise their own price as they want the prospect to choose the competitor because they are confident that their competition will lose money on this customer weakening them for future competitive conquests. To the customer, Progressive looks like the "good guy." Using advanced analytics to make major decisions, Progressive has automated 97.5 % of all decisions and has helped to propel Progressive to a spot as one of the top three insurers in the USA. Progressive has been referred to as a data company that happens to be in the insurance industry.

Another firm known as USAA takes a leadership role in the use of advanced analytics for insurance cross-selling. Formed in 1922 by retired army officers who could not obtain insurance through traditional channels, this firm has chosen to only provide insurance and other financial services to US military personnel. With its finite market niche, USAA has not traditionally focused on market share but instead has remained focused on share of wallet. In fact, *USAA* tracks *wallet share* and retention rates separately by life-stage segment. In addition, USAA uses advanced modeling to know their customer base extremely well following marriages, births, retirements, and other life-changing patterns, so it can advise customers on changing needs. Responding to these patterns through advanced algorithms, USAA increases revenues by selling more insurance and financial services. It also increases customer satisfaction and loyalty by monitoring and adapting to their needs. While competitors look to cut costs by reducing direct customer contact, USAA encourages members to phone in and prepares its service reps for interactions. As a result, member loyalty fuels consistent annual growth of USAA's—asset and member bases. Today, 5.6 million USAA members live in 4.5 million households, and they own almost 22 million USAA products, an average of nearly five per household. With a marketable universe of <10 % of the US population in a fiercely competitive arena, USAA has become a Fortune 500 company with over $13B in annual revenues.

So I hope you are now convinced that advanced analytics have now begun to reach the business mainstream. Recently, I sit on an analytics panel with many top Fortune 500 firms. When I started in the analytics field over 20 years ago, there were only a few companies out there which made extensive use of analytics besides insurance whose whole business model hinges upon embedded analytics (although a full customer analytics approach is still lacking throughout the industry). These were consumer finance and pharmaceuticals.

The other proof that advanced analytics are getting more important for the successful operation of firms is a popular book on analytics by Davenport called Competing on Analytics. Also, the precursor to this book was the most downloaded article ever in the Harvard Business Review. Another popular book on the subject is titled Super Crunchers written by Ian Ayers. Finally, there have been several recent articles in popular business media including BusinessWeek and the Economist.

As businesses compete on the basis of analytics, they will need to have even more advanced algorithms to be able to compete successfully. In essence, it becomes a form of analytic arms race with firms competing in defined markets with more powerful algorithms from which to understand and retain their own customers or attract new ones from the competition.

The proof that this concept of advanced analytics is necessary can be found in the extensive use of algorithms by modern firms. High-speed computing and data storage improvements have made this possible to firms of all types. Netflix, for example, uses specialized algorithms to determine your movie preferences. Similarly, Amazon.com uses algorithms to generate recommendations for other titles and iTunes uses algorithms which begin to determine one's music preferences starting from the first time one downloads a song. Not only do these algorithms improve the current sales and profitability of these firms, but they also guarantee future profitability by being more customer centric. This all used to fall under the umbrella of CRM or customer relationship management. The central premise of CRM is that there is a targeted strategy for each customer depending on their past behavior and characteristics. The major movement moving toward this strategy began in the early 1980s. However, after the financial crisis which began in 2008, many firms have moved away from a targeted strategy for all customers and replaced it with a targeted strategy for only the most profitable customers. This process pioneered by Gary Loveland when he became the CEO of Harrah's is known as customer value management or CVM. CVM is the art and science of managing customer value and can be a much more efficient strategy than the popular CRM strategies.

Since these firms depend on algorithms to compete, it goes without saying that the better we can make these algorithms perform, the better they will be able to compete in the global marketplace.

The face of *CRM analytics* in consumer finance industry has changed dramatically with the advent of increased computing power along with an array of statistical tools serving the purpose more than expected. The modern CRM research has organized itself along the line of *customer life cycle*, including customer *acquisition*, *development*, and *retention strategies*. The retention of customers is increasingly becoming more expensive especially in service-based industries such as telecommunications and financial services (Davenport and Harris 2007). This has led to the need for more effective consumer attrition scoring.

As mentioned earlier, the retention of customers is increasingly becoming more expensive especially in service-based industries such as telecommunications and financial services (Davenport and Harris 2007). Further research is necessary to be able to apply this model to various retention applications in these industries which could then potentially contribute to making the retention of customers significantly more economical.

While high-speed computers and the expansion of electronic commerce have increased the need and use of advanced analytical algorithms, there is also an establishment who depends on traditional heuristics that works to slow the progress of advancement in these areas. In the modern corporation, it is the employees that typically do not understand the nature of analytics and have been successful at making decisions based on gut feelings who are typically resistant to progress. There is no example of resistance in this area more prevalent than in the critique of fine wines. Orley Ashenfelter, a Princeton economist and wine connoisseur, has developed an algorithm which can predict the general quality of any wine vintage by plugging the weather statistics for a given year into his algorithm. This is actually prediction which challenges the after-the-fact process of using the "swishing and spitting" approach of wine gurus. Ashenfelter's algorithms have proven to be very accurate at predicting the quality of vintages in the Bordeaux region of France; however, traditional wine critics and the Bordeaux wine industry have resisted his predictions making comments on his work ranging from "somewhere between violent and hysterical…the reasoning is that this threatens the very assumptions that have developed over the years of how vintage wines should be properly assessed" (Ayres 2007).

Advanced analytics at first blush sound intimidating to the non-mathematician. However, the algorithms which have resulted for advanced analysis have become quite common in a host of business transactions. For instance, every time you swipe a credit card, a whole host of algorithms are executed which depend on the amount purchased and the type of transaction as inputs and which then are used to generate additional offers to the customer to further build balances and credit card utilization. In addition to the traditional variables utilized in actuarial tables to determine insurance premiums, insurance companies are increasingly reliant upon credit scoring to determine the relative risk of a potential customer. Some people question the efficacy of this, given that insurance is different than credit products. However, companies like Progressive insurance and others have proven quantitatively that these algorithms are related to insurance claims and fraud. UPS uses advanced algorithms to help deliver hundreds of millions of packages per year to their destination in the most efficient manner possible. With all the destinations and routes available to drivers, it is virtually impossible for the human mind to comprehend all of this. Algorithms are therefore needed to make these important decisions. Advanced analytics are definitely not for everyone. The use of them depends to a large extent on how much data the concerned companies generate. For instance, credit card companies with daily transaction data use advanced analytics more frequently than insurance companies with annual renewals. Some will also be more focused than others on how advanced analytics can save costs or maximize capacity. Hau Lee of Stanford Graduate School of Business explained that firms that enjoy high margins and strong demand are going to be less worried about the efficiency of their supply chains (Business by Numbers 2007).

So what are the things that firms need to have in place for advanced analytics to work? Firstly, advanced analytics by their nature tend to be highly complex: It is not easy to find people with the right skills to develop and refine them. Also, the systems within which the advanced analytics run—the user interface—need to be intuitive to non-experts. Moreover, the inputs have to be right. Did the firm take measures to properly deal with missing or unreliable data? Finally, with advanced analytics in place within the firm, human judgment still has to have a role. An example of this is in credit card fraud detection systems where algorithms including neural networks can approve and process the majority of transactions, but a human is still best placed to analyze the difficult ones (Business by Numbers 2007).

The late Ronald Fisher who is considered to be the father of modern statistics provided a focal point for statistical methods at the outset of his famous 1922 article:

> …the objective of statistical methods is the reduction of data. A quantity of data is to be replaced by relatively few quantities which shall adequately represent the relevant information contained in the original data.Since the number of independent facts supplied in the data is usually far greater than the number of facts sought, much of the information supplied by an actual sample is irrelevant. It is the object of the statistical process employed in the reduction of data to exclude this irrelevant information, and to isolate the whole of the relevant information contained in the data (Fisher 1922).

In these statements, Fisher signified the goal of statistical methods to filter out the irrelevant information and only to give out the relevant information. In spite of all the hype in the media on the future of advanced analytics taking the place of human decision making, there is instead something more basic going on here. That is in our environment of ever-increasing complexity and data, the main purpose of these more powerful methods is to continue to fulfill the main role outlined by Fisher many decades ago. Therefore, it is important that we continue to embrace and support the development of advanced statistical methods to insure that we can continue to extract the relevant information from the vast oceans of data we are collecting in our society.

The purpose of writing this book is to train the next generation of business analysts and managers about the power of analytics with its unique ability as a function to identify and provide solutions to inherent inefficiencies of decision making through human judgments alone. Critics may try to de-emphasize the current role of analytics by pointing out companies which used to have a reputation for being data driven but have now fallen in performance. However, being analytic driven does not mean that firms can rest on their laurels and no longer have to innovate. The preponderance of Big Data from initiatives such as the "Internet of Things" for industry and social, local, and mobile (SOLOMO) for services will allow all firms, even those who are already sophisticated analytically, to jump the S-curve.

Each individual chapter of this book was written in the attempt to allow analysts and managers to have a firm base for making data-driven decisions on a major function of a firm, While no book can cover all of the possibilities to deploy analytics in a firm implementing some of the techniques and learning from each of these chapters will allow analysts and managers to take their organizations to the next level where they become analytical competitors in the marketplace rather than a firm which simply performs analytics.

Chapters 2 and 3 focus on a principle that every business knows, but few actually do something about which is the fact that it is easier and less expensive to retain and nourish existing customers than it is to acquire new ones. In a world where customers have immediate access to information about competitor's products and services, implementing the learning from this chapter will allow firms to stop the leak and focus on delighting their customers, so they share their experiences via word of mouth.

Chapter 4 focuses on make better decisions on advertising branding and media spend which for many companies is their biggest marketing expense and is treated as an art rather than a science. Taking the learning from this chapter will allow analysts and managers to bridge the gap between art and science and start attributing marketing activity and investments to actual business outcomes. This will serve to enhance the position of the modern chief marketing officer who is under increasing pressure to deliver solid results.

Chapters 5 and 8 are geared toward retail firms who are experiencing a major transition with the Internet and consolidation. Retailers with their loyalty programs were among the first types of firms to be truly data driven, but their techniques are a bit stale and need to be refreshed. Taking the learning from this chapter will allow analysts and managers to compete on analytics in the modern world by updating some of the very techniques which made many retailers analytical competitors in the past. While the examples in these two chapters are primarily retail focused, there are still lessons to be learned in deploying advanced analytics to all types of businesses.

Chapter 6 was written in attempt to help firms use an analytic approach to acquiring new customers. Customer acquisition remains a big expense for many firms and one with diminishing returns as competitors frequently catch up and alternative distribution channels proliferate. Taking the lessons from Chap. 5 will enable business managers and analysts to reverse the declining trends and increase their return on acquisition.

Chapters 7 and 9 will focus on one of the most critical roles of marketing which is pricing a firm's products and/or services. In simulations where managers are given pricing decisions against other managers in which they are passionate about competing against all of these managers tended to drop their own prices in response to competitive pressures regardless of the perceived quality of their products or services. Chapters 6 and 8 focus on how managers can use science rather than emotions to set the prices of their products based on solid analytics and design of experiments.

Chapter 10 will focus on advanced data mining techniques which can change the game for businesses who compete on analytics against competitors who are using standard parametric and nonparametric statistical techniques developed in a world where massive amounts of data and computing power exist. Statistics show that there has been more data collected over the last few years than collectively in decades preceding. Furthermore, the modern PC has more computing power than NASA systems used to send men to the moon. Businesses which desire to take advantage of these resources and can often look to nature as a way to solve new problems. Ant colony optimization is one such new technique introduced in Chap. 10 which businesses can adopt to help make better decisions. The benefits of following nature when designing decision support systems and the algorithms obtained within is its had millions of years to perfect the process.

Chapter 11 is a capstone chapter which will put all of the techniques above into service to focus on analytics techniques critical for customer life cycle management. Many firms such as television networks and pharmaceutical firms have products and services which customers will use throughout their lifetime. Customer lifetime value is a buzzword which is currently thrown out there as the answer to the challenges of keeping a customer throughout their lives. However, firms should be less focused on future value and more focused on life cycle management, so their customers will be able to have the right products and services as they reach each new stage in their lives. Following the lessons from Chap. 10 will enable firms to develop a relationship with their customers throughout their lifetimes and build customer loyalty over time.

References

Analyze This (2006) Security. SecurityMagazine.com. Accessed 5 Oct 2007

Ayres I (2007) Super crunchers: why thinking-by-numbers is the new way to be smart. Bantam Dell Publishing Group

Bauer K (2006) Predictive analytics: algorithm nirvana. Direct marketing review, pp 40–49

Bernstein PL (1998) Against the Gods: the remarkable story of risk. John Wiley and Sons, Inc., New York

Bhaskar T, Sundararajan R, Atherill P, Fogarty D (2007) A genetic algorithm for building propensity models. J Direct Mark

Britt P (2007) Advanced analytics offer greater precision. Speech Technol 12(4):32–35

"Business by Numbers" The Economist, 15 Sept 2007, pp 81–83

Cacchione T (2006) Advanced analytics make for smarter claims decisions, improve bottom line. National underwriter: property and casualty, pp 26–27

Chen YK, Yeh AC (2004) An enhancement of DSI_X control charts using a Fuzzy-genetic approach. Int J Adv Manuf Technol 24(10):32–40

Cole M (2007) Scott Boras, The Uber-Agent Uses Data-Mining to Attract Baseball Talent. Businesweek, Sept 26, pp 58–59

Coyne FJ (2007) Harnessing analytics. Best's Review 107(10): 74

Davenport TH, Harris JG (2007) Competing on analytics: the new science of winning. Harvard Business School Press

Drummond MF, Sculpher MJ (2006) Better analysis for better decisions: facing up to the challenges. Pharmacoeconomics 24(11):1039–1042

Efron B (2008) The future of statistics. Amstat News 363:47–50

Fisher RA (1922) On the mathematical foundations of statistics, Philos Trans Roy Ser A 222: 309–366

Fogarty DJ (2001) Intelligent imputation: a new methodology for data quality management on commercial data warehouses. Published PhD. Dissertation, British National Library

INA ARTICL Datamonitor SAS Institute Inc. http://www.datamonitor.com/~9194df270b884b558a5f2781c89ad1ee~/

Kimball R (2002) Behavior: the next marquee application; it's time to start using more advanced analytics. Intell Enterp 26(3):28

Krol C (2006) Demand grows for analytics. B to B 91(1):16

McMillan DJ, Beiko RG, Geffers R, Buer J, Schouls LM, Vlaminckx BJM, Wannet JB, Sriprakash KS, Chhatwal GS (2006) Genes for the majority of group a streptococcal virulence factors and extracellular surface proteins do not confer an increased propensity to cause invasive disease. Clinical infectious diseases, pp 884–891

Monash CA (2005) Milking Moore's Law. ComputerWorld, p 32

Monch L, Stehl M, Zimmerman J, Habenicht I (2006) The FABMAS multi-agent prototype for production control of water fabs: design, implementation and performance assessment. Prod Plann Control 17(7):701–716

Oplatkova Z, Zelinka I (2006) Santa fe trail for artificial ant with analytic programming and three evolutionary algorithms. In: Proceedings of the first Asia international conference on modelling and simulation, pp 450–456

Pham TD, Tran DT, Zho X, Wong ST (2006) Integrated algorithms for image analysis and classification of nuclear division for high-content cell-cycle screening. Int J Comput Intell Appl 6(1):21–43

Reimers BD (2000) Getting personal–advanced analytics can help e-businesses land customers. Information Week, pp 51–52

Seybor J (2007) From crayons to calculators. Customer Relat Manag 11(1):26

Tani M (ed) (2007) Arizona utility selects PCI for portfolio optimization and advanced analytics. Transmission & Distribution World, p 23

Tucker A, Hoen P, Vinciotti V, Liu X (2006) Temporal Bayesian classifiers for modelling muscular dystrophy expression data. Intell Data Anal 10(4):441–455

Chapter 2
Severity of Dormancy Model (SDM): Reckoning the Customers Before They Quiescent

Saumitra N. Bhaduri, S. Raja Sethu Durai and David Fogarty

Abstract The chapter proposes a severity of dormancy model (SDM), which allows the potential dormancy and the extent of dormancy to be modeled separately and is attempted for one of the key retail businesses for a large European business. The methodology developed in this chapter challenges the conventional wisdom of building a dormancy model using a logistic regression technique. It recognizes the existence of a group of potential dormant customer who would never go dormant under any circumstances. Most importantly, it not only recognizes this subset of customers, but also explicitly models the probability of the extent of dormancy to depend on customer attributes. Finally, the chapter successfully demonstrates the improvement achieved by the SDM over the conventional technique to capture the severity of dormancy.

2.1 Introduction

The face of CRM analytics in consumer finance industry has changed dramatically with the advent of increased computing power along with an array of statistical tools serving the purpose more than expected. The modern CRM research has organized itself along the line of customer life cycle, including customer acquisition, development, and retention strategies. However, the recent years have witnessed a strategic shift toward maximizing the lifetime value of the customers by retaining the existing one than acquiring new. The research has shown that the customer retention has a significant impact on firm profitability: Gupta et al. (2004) find that 1 % improvement in retention leads to an increase of firm value by 5 %. Therefore, the focus of CRM research has been to exactly identify the factors of dormancy at a particular point in time as it helps the firm to design strategies to serve the customer better in order to prevent inactivity. The primary objective of consumer dormancy scoring has therefore been to develop methods and techniques to precisely identify the potential attrition in a cost-effective manner.

This chapter contains contributions from S. Raja Sethu Durai, Madras School of Economics, Chennai, India.

S.N. Bhaduri and D. Fogarty, *Advanced Business Analytics*,
DOI 10.1007/978-981-10-0727-9_2

Historically, first-generation models have dominated the CRM analytics scenario, in which the consumer-scoring methods are aimed at classifying customers into "good" and "bad" defection classes according to their probability to go dormant by a given time in the future. Several different modeling techniques have been attempted to develop such classifier discriminant analysis, logistic regression, partitioning tree, mathematical programming, neural networks, expert systems and genetic algorithms, Markov chain, and to mention a few. Survey chapters by Hand and Henley (1997), Rosenberg and Gleit (1994), Thomas (1998) provide a useful summary of such techniques. However, despite the plethora of such techniques, logistic regression has become the workhorse in scorecard developments. Albeit its simplicity and reasonable prediction power for discrete events, logistic regression (and other similar classifier) has significant disadvantages. Therefore, the first-generation models have served a significant value addition to businesses but often pose a significant conceptual and implementation challenges. Firstly, these models primarily focus on the "outcome" of an economic process, e.g., attrition, dormancy, payoff, or retention and hence completely ignore the data-generating process behind the consumer behavior. Second is the absence of endogenous "cost–benefit analysis" for the proposed model. Most often or not, these models are implemented with an ad hoc average estimate of cost or benefits. Therefore, without an estimate of "customer level loss or benefit," it tends to overestimate or underestimate the potential benefit of the proposed model.

A major limitation of logistic regression (and other similar classifier) is that it ignores the simple observation that customers go dormant with different balance characteristics in their life cycle and hence undermines the dynamic element in customer inactive behavior. Therefore, as we explore the dynamic element in the inactive behavior, one questions not if a customer would go dormant, but if they, what would be the cost to the business from loosing the customer? Though this is a far more difficult question than to provide a binary answer of yes/no, it has several distinct advantages: The expected loss of balance from dormancy can be a better indicator to design retention strategy than a simple potential dormancy probability. Customer with higher expected loss of balance can be far more important than identifying the potential dormant customer (possibly with low expect balance), as these events might not have symmetric consequences for firm's profitability.

The chapter is, therefore, an attempt to introduce a second-generation models that aim at developing an "optimization technique" such that the "cost–benefit analysis" of the proposed strategy becomes endogenous to the modeling process. With it establishes a robust model in identifying the outcome along with the extent of cost or benefit associated with the proposed selection.

The chapter develops a Severity of Dormancy Model (SDM) using a two-stage framework for a retail portfolio of a large European firm. The chapter is organized as follows: Sect. 2.2 gives a brief literature on two-stage model and discusses the methodology proposed in this chapter. Section 2.3 narrates the description of the data used. Section 2.4 provides the results. Section 2.5 compares the results of the SDM with the conventional dormancy model based on logistic regression. Finally, the conclusions are provided in Sect. 2.6.

2.2 Severity of Dormancy Model

The chapter argues that dormancy occurs only when customer becomes inactive for a long period of time, but for any dormancy can become costly to the business if two conditions are satisfied: first, an incident with positive probability of dormancy and second, a higher expected loss of balance due to dormancy. Number of studies have followed suit by using a similar structure of model in various aspects from estimating cigarette consumption (Jones 1989) to wildlife valuation (Espineira 2004). On the credit scoring front, Dionne et al. (1996) argued that estimating the default probabilities is not sufficient for appropriate evaluation of credit scoring and proposed a similar model. Moffat (2005) used a double hurdle model to estimate loan default.

2.2.1 *Methodology*

As the name suggests, a consumer in this framework must cross two stages in order be dormant (Cragg 1971). The "first stage" needs to be crossed in order to be a potential dormant. Given that the customer is a potential dormant, his expect loss of balance would then dictate whether or not he will in fact go dormant—the "second stage."

2.2.2 *Severity of Dormancy Model*

The model contains two equations. We write as follows:

$$\begin{aligned} d_i^* &= z_i'\alpha + \varepsilon_i \\ y_i^{**} &= x_i'\beta + u_i \end{aligned}$$

$$\begin{pmatrix} \varepsilon_i \\ u_i \end{pmatrix} \sim N\left[\begin{pmatrix} 0 \\ 0 \end{pmatrix}, \begin{pmatrix} 1 & 0 \\ 0 & \sigma^2 \end{pmatrix}\right] \tag{2.1}$$

Note from the diagonality of the covariance matrix that the two error terms are assumed to be independently distributed.

The first stage is then represented by:

$$\begin{aligned} d_i &= 1 \quad \text{if } d_i^* \geq 0 \\ d_i &= 0 \quad \text{if } d_i^* \leq 0 \end{aligned} \tag{2.2}$$

Equation (2.2) is therefore close to a Probit representation. The second stage closely resembles the Tobit model with the following specification.

$$y_i^* = x_i'\beta + u_i \quad i = 1, \Lambda, n$$

$$u_i \sim N(0, \sigma^2) \tag{2.3}$$

where y_i^* is a latent variable representing the borrower i's propensity to go dormant, x_i is a vector of a borrower characteristics relevant in explaining the extent of dormancy, β is a corresponding vector of parameters to be estimated, and u_i is a homoscedastic, normally distributed error term. Let y_i be the severity of dormancy. The chapter defines a customer to be dormant if he generates at least 6 consecutive zero balances and remains zero till the end of the performance window. The dormant month is defined as the month at which a dormant customer hits his/her first zero. The dormant month will range from 1 to 7 in our sample. The severity of dormancy is defined as SevDor = [1 − (Dormant Month/12)]. For example, if the dormant month = 1, then SevDor = 1 − (1/12) = 0.916, while for non-dormant accounts, SevDor is zero. A customer goes dormant in the first month bears higher severity than the customer goes dormant in the seventh month. The severity of dormancy

Since severity of dormancy cannot be negative, the relationship between y_i^* and y_i is as follows:

$$y_i = \max(y_i^*, 0) \tag{2.4}$$

Equation (2.4) gives rise to the standard censored regression model widely known as Tobit model. The log-likelihood function for the Tobit model is given as follows:

$$\text{Log}\,L = \sum_0 \text{In}\left[1 - \Phi\left(\frac{x_i'\beta}{\sigma}\right)\right] + \sum_+ \text{In}\left[\frac{1}{\sigma}\phi\left(\frac{y_i - x_i'\beta}{\sigma}\right)\right] \tag{2.5}$$

in which "0" indicates summation over the zero observations in the sample, while "+" indicates summation over positive observations. $\Phi(\cdot)$ and $\phi(\cdot)$ are the standard normal cdf and pdf, respectively.

Finally, the observed variable y_i in the severity of dormancy model is determined as follows:

$$y_i = d_i y_i^* \tag{2.7}$$

The log-likelihood function for the two-stage model is as follows:

$$\text{Log}\,L = \sum_0 \text{In}\left[1 - \Phi(z_i'\alpha)\Phi\left(\frac{x_i'\beta}{\sigma}\right)\right] + \sum_+ \text{In}\left[\Phi(z_i'\alpha)\frac{1}{\sigma}\phi\left(\frac{y_i - x_i'\beta}{\sigma}\right)\right] \tag{2.8}$$

The model predicts the estimated loss of balance as a potential balance multiplied by estimated SevDor, where potential balance is defined as a last three-month average balance multiplied by the length of the performance window of twelve months.

A diagram (2.1) below may be useful for understanding the model. The maximum likelihood estimation is applied to estimate α and β jointly along with the σ.

2.2.3 *Prediction*

Estimating the predicted values of d_i and y_i* is as important as estimating the α and β. The predictions are constructed in two steps as follows: From the estimated α coefficient, the probability of attrition is calculated, which is similar to that of a probability of attrition from a typical Probit model.

The severity of dormancy is then calculated as follows:

$$\hat{y}_i = \Phi(x_i'\beta/\sigma) * \left\{x_i'\beta + \sigma * \left(\frac{\phi(x_i'\beta/\sigma)}{\Phi(x_i'\beta/\sigma)}\right)\right\}$$

Finally, the expected severity of dormancy is given as follows: $\hat{p}(\text{Dormancy}) * \hat{y}_i$.

2.2.4 *Estimation*

There is no standard routine available in SAS to estimate this severity of dormancy model. One needs to write a program using maximum likelihood routine PROC NLMIXED available in SAS. The SAS program used to estimate the model described in this chapter is shown in the appendix.

2.3 Data

Retail data of a large European business have been used in this study. Total number of observation is 187,300 of which dormant accounts are 40,511, which is 21 % of the population. The 5.8 % of population was partially dormant and hence excluded from the sample. Out of 176,614 sampled accounts, we further split it into 70:30 as development and validation sample. Final set of development sample has 124,091 observations and the validation sample has 54,030 observations. A careful look into the dormancy pattern will reveal that a reasonable number of accounts do come back after six months of inactivity. To accommodate this possibility of higher inactive period in the data, we have modified the dormancy definition as a string of six consecutive zero balance and remain zero till the end of performance window (Fig. 2.1).

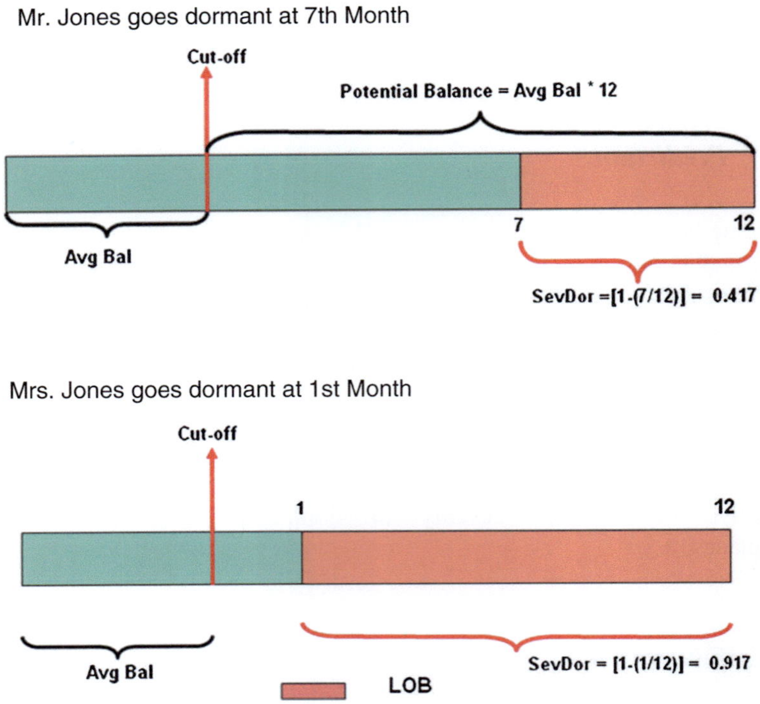

Fig. 2.1 Severity of dormancy model

Table 2.1 The sample for the SDM

Total accounts	187,300	
Dormant accounts	40,511	21.63 %
Partial dormant accounts	12,229	6.53 %
Non-dormant accounts	137,646	73.49 %
Data used in the model		
Total accounts	176,614	
Dormant accounts	40,511	22.94 %
Non-dormant accounts	137,646	77.94 %

These numbers clearly indicate that the dormancy is a big concern to worry and an effective strategy to identify the severity of dormancy will hold the key to prevent it through customized strategies (Tables 2.1 and 2.2).

Table 2.2 Dormancy structure

		Zero balance for consecutive months				
		2	3	4	5	6
Coming back months	3	35.6				
	4	31.9	27.1			
	5	29.4	23.7	20.1		
	6	24.7	19.5	16.1	13.3	
	7	18.3	14.5	11.7	10.1	9.1
	8	15.5	11.6	9.3	7.7	6.7
	9	14.4	10.2	7.9	6.3	5.4
	10	13.0	8.8	6.3	4.9	4.1
	11	11.5	8.2	5.5	3.8	3.1
	12	8.4	6.2	4.5	2.8	1.9

2.4 Variables Used

The study uses all the terminated accounts as of July 2006. The data consist of transaction information from July 2004 to July 2006. The observation window is defined from July 2004 to July 2005, while the next 12 months constitute the performance window. For the model, a dormancy flag has been created. The flag takes the value of zero if the accounts are non-dormant and one otherwise. Also, we compute an additional variables namely severity of dormancy (SevDor as: For the accounts that have been dormant, SevDor is defined as SevDor = [1 − (Dormant Month/12)]. For all the non-dormant accounts, it is by definition takes a value of zero.

The selections of independent variables in the model are carried out after checking for correlation and multicollinearity. Finally, a robustness checks have been performed for the proposed mode using the validation sample.

2.5 Results

The estimates of the model proposed in this chapter are reported in Table 2.3. The sample size used in the estimation is 124,091. All the variables included in the model are significant at 99.99 % level. Selection of variables is done through a routine multicollinearity check, having all VIFs less than 1.75. Focusing on the explanatory variables, such as utilization, trends in balance, purchase frequency, and recency, seems to influence the first stage. Also a set of demographic variables such as age have a strong influence on the first stage. It is interesting to note that the second stage is influenced by a different set of explanatory variables (different dummies), thereby justifying our choice of our SDM.

Table 2.3 Severity of dormancy model estimates

Variable	Definition	Estimate	SE	*t*-value	Prob
First stage					
Intercept		−0.0767	0.0030	−25.9	<0.0001
Point2util	Utilization at cutoff point	−0.0023	0.0001	−39.6	<0.0001
CLIM_2	Credit limit at cutoff point	0.0000	0.0000	−54.7	<0.0001
inbal3	OBSBAL_12 > OBSBAL_11 > OBSBAL_10	−0.0322	0.0026	−12.4	<0.0001
Dumutil	(Change of utilization) > 0	0.0366	0.0023	16.1	<0.0001
Diffbal	(Change of balance) > 0	−0.0212	0.0025	−8.5	<0.0001
d3_age	33 < age ≤ 43	−0.0099	0.0022	−4.5	<0.0001
d5_age	Age > 53	0.0248	0.0021	11.7	<0.0001
d1_ABAL_9	Average BAL_9 ≤ 0	0.2250	0.0162	13.9	<0.0001
d2_ABAL_9	0 < average BAL_9 ≤ 15.78	0.1868	0.0025	74.6	<0.0001
d5_PURFR_6	Purchase frequency last 6 months > 8	−0.1143	0.0029	−40.0	<0.0001
d1_PURRE	Purchase RECENCY ≤ 13	−0.0626	0.0023	−27.0	<0.0001
d4_PURRE	54 < purchase RECENCY ≤ 216	−0.0123	0.0023	−5.4	<0.0001
d4_MOB	MOB > 114	−0.0167	0.0024	−7.1	<0.0001
Sigma		0.0380	0.0002	230.7	<0.0001
Second stage					
Intercept		0.1274	0.0004	334.2	<0.0001
dum_3	OBSBAL_09 = OBSBAL_10 = OBSBAL_11 = 0	0.0052	0.0006	9.0	<0.0001
Czero	No of consecutive zeros	0.0021	0.0001	25.5	<0.0001
d5_PURFR_6	Purchase frequency in last 6 months > 8	−0.0099	0.0010	−9.8	<0.0001
d4_ABAL_9	43.86 < average BAL_9 ≤ 81.34	−0.0047	0.0007	−6.3	<0.0001

Note Any further description of the independent variables cannot be provided due to the confidentiality agreement with data provider

2.6 Beyond Conventional Dormancy Model

The received wisdom of developing a dormancy model is to estimate the probability of early dormancy using a logistic regression technique. Since we are also interested in identifying the extent of dormancy, we developed a SDM in which the dormancy probability is estimated using a Probit model and SevDor been estimated using a Tobit model.

This section compares the strategy of using a conventional attrition model with a SDM proposed in this chapter to exactly recognize the additional improvement achieved by SDM over the traditional logistic regression. To make a successful comparison, we adopt a three-step strategy: (a) We build a dormancy model using a conventional logistic regression. The estimates of dormancy model are reported in Table 2.4. (b) Develop a strategy based on the logistics model: Select only top five deciles. (c) Compare the result with a SDM strategy.

Table 2.4 presents the estimates of conventional logistic regression-based dormancy model. Model explains the dormancy behavior reasonably for the sample as indicated by a high concordance level. The rank order presented in Table 2.5 also shows the validity of the model as top five deciles capture 80 % of the dormant customer.

All the variables included in the model are also statistically significant. However, the conventional dormancy performs poorly in capturing the extent of dormancy defined as actual loss of balance (LOB). Here, the LOB is the difference between the potential balance and the actual balance in the target window. The potential balance is calculated as 12 multiplied by the average monthly balance in the last 3 months in the observation window, and actual balance is sum of the balances in the target window. The Table 2.6 shows that top five deciles only capture 33 % of LOB of dormant accounts with average monthly LOB of £39.

Therefore, the conventional model has significant power in correctly identifying the dormant customers, but lacks in establishing the extent of dormancy as well as the loss of balance associated with it. One of the possible reasons for such perverse result is the fact that model assignees low probability of dormancy to accounts with high average balance (negative coefficient), which naturally pushes down the high loss of balance accounts to the bottom of the deciles. In contrast, the SDM provides additional information on estimated loss of balance over the conventional model. With that, it establishes a robust model in identifying the dormant people along with the extent of dormancy and its associated loss of balance.

Table 2.4 Logistic regression results for development sample

Variable	Definition	Estimate	SE	Chi-Sq	Prob
Intercept		−0.518	0.0260	420.1	<0.0001
Point2util	Utilization at cutoff point	−0.006	0.0006	1508.1	<0.0001
CLIM_2	Credit limit at cutoff point	0.015	0.0000	3123.1	<0.0001
inbal3	OBSBAL_12 > OBSBAL_11 > OBSBAL_10	−0.299	0.0240	171.2	<0.0001
Dumutil	(Change in utilization) > 0	0.347	0.0201	270.6	<0.0001
Diffbal	(Change in balance) > 0	−0.198	0.0225	90.5	<0.0001
d3_age	33 < age ≤ 43	−0.079	0.0198	22.8	<0.0001
d5_age	Age > 54	0.239	0.0186	145.2	<0.0001
d1_ABAL_9	ABAL_9 ≤ 0	1.181	0.1304	79.8	<0.0001
d2_ABAL_9	0 < ABAL_9 ≤ 15.78	1.489	0.0209	4990.4	<0.0001
d5_PURFR_6	Purchase frequency in last 6 months > 8	−1.160	0.0291	1628.3	<0.0001
d1_PURRE	Purchase RECENCY ≤ 13	−0.553	0.0212	722.6	<0.0001
d4_PURRE	54 < purchase RECENCY ≤ 216	−0.100	0.0203	32.5	<0.0001
d4_MOB	MOB > 114	−0.132	0.0213	47.9	<0.0001
Percent concordant	79.3	Somers' D	0.588		
Percent discordant	20.4	Gamma	0.590		
Percent tied	0.3	Tau-*a*	0.203		
Pairs	2,598,259,968	*c*	0.794		

Note Any further description of the independent variables cannot be provided due to the confidentiality agreement with data provider

Table 2.5 Conventional dormancy model (logistic regression), total sample

Total LOB						
Decile	Non-dormant	Cum freq (%)	Dormant	Cum freq (%)	Partial dormant	Cum freq (%)
1	3964	3	11,422	29	3189	30
2	8499	9	7558	49	2519	53
3	11,625	18	5307	62	1644	69
4	13,590	28	3,736,159	72	675,132	79
5	14,984	39	4,135,791	80	612,450	85
6	15,797	50	4,739,064	86	654,432	90
7	16,019	62	5,379,414	91	756,572	94
8	16,689	74	5,625,126	95	660,716	97
9	17,321	87	5,298,688	98	572,558	99
10	17,615	100	8,207,652	100	1,154,352	100
Total	136,103		38,968		10,686	

Table 2.6 Loss of balance captured by the conventional dormancy model (logistic regression), total sample

Total LOB						
Decile	Non-dormant	Cum freq (%)	Dormant	Cum freq (%)	Partial dormant	Cum freq (%)
1	−767,147	3	1,501,522	3	260,742	4
2	−2,044,811	10	1,863,315	8	426,796	11
3	−2,257,120	17	3,192,419	15	700,439	21
4	−3,484,151	29	3,736,159	24	675,132	32
5	−3,932,015	43	4,135,791	33	612,450	41
6	−3,010,180	53	4,739,064	44	654,432	51
7	−3,680,107	66	5,379,414	56	756,572	63
8	−2,187,203	74	5,625,126	69	660,716	73
9	569,724	72	5,298,688	81	572,558	82
10	−8,254,953	100	8,207,652	100	1,154,352	100
Total	−29,047,963		43,679,150		6,474,189	

The ex-post distribution of the accounts targeted though the SDM is reported in Table 2.7. The ex-post distribution presented in Table 2.7 clearly demonstrates the power of SDM as the top five deciles capture 86 % of LOB of dormant accounts with average monthly LOB of €203. Further, the same findings are corroborated by the holdout sample.

Table 2.7 Loss of balance captured by the SDM, total sample

Total LOB						
Decile	Non-dormant	Cum freq (%)	Dormant	Cum freq (%)	Partial dormant	Cum freq (%)
1	13,759,165	−47	14,665,702	34	1,636,643	25
2	380,661	−49	7,706,133	51	964,769	40
3	−2,684,010	−39	6,949,157	67	1,092,300	57
4	−5,237,190	−21	4,789,627	78	902,789	71
5	−5,199,342	−4	3,612,709	86	690,724	82
6	−4,774,331	13	2,420,636	92	580,475	91
7	−5,435,254	32	1,596,380	96	333,876	96
8	−5,624,630	51	1,148,792	98	217,446	99
9	−6,449,766	73	689,137	100	92,611	101
10	−7,783,265	100	100,877	100	−37,443	100
Total	−29,047,962		43,679,150		6,474,190	

2.7 Conclusions

The chapter develops a Severity of Dormancy Model that challenges the conventional wisdom of building a dormancy model using a logistic regression technique. The methodology developed in this chapter clearly recognizes the existence of a group of potential dormant customer who would never attrite under any circumstances. Most importantly, the SDM not only recognizes existence of this group of customer but also explicitly models the probability of actual dormancy to depend on customer attributes. Finally, the model successfully demonstrates a significant improvement over the conventional technique by capturing the extent of dormancy through loss of outstanding balance.

References

Cragg JG (1971) Some statistical models for limited dependent variables with application to the demand for durable goods. Econometrica 39(5):829–844

Dionne G, Artis M, Guillen M (1996) Count data models for a credit scoring system. J Empir Finance 3(3):303–325

Espineira RM (2004) A box-cox double-hurdle model of wildlife valuation: the citizen's perspective. IN: Chapter presented on the Sixth Annual BIOECON Conference held at Kings College Cambridge, 2–3 Sept 2004

Gupta S, Lehmann D, Stuart J (2004) Valuing customers. J Mark Res 41(1):7–18

Hand DJ, Henley WE (1997) Statistical classification methods in consumer credit. J R Stat Soc Series A 160:523–541

Jones A (1989) A double-Hurdle model of cigarette consumption. J Appl Econ 4(1):23–39
Moffat P (2005) Hurdle models of loan default. J Oper Res Soc 56:1063–1071
Rosenberg E, Gleit A (1994) Quantitative methods in credit management: a survey. Oper Res 42:589–613
Thomas LC (1998) Methodology for classifying applicants for credit" statistics in finance. Edward Arnold, London, pp 83–103

Chapter 3
Double Hurdle Model: Not if, but When Will Customer Attrite?

Saumitra N. Bhaduri, S. Raja Sethu Durai and David Fogarty

Abstract Similar to the SDM, this chapter attempts to introduce a class of model known as double hurdle models (originally proposed by Cragg (1971)), which allows the potential attrition and the extent of attrition to be modeled separately. This double hurdle model of attrition is attempted for a European auto finance portfolio. The methodology developed in this chapter identifies a group of potential attritor who would never attrite under any circumstances. Most importantly, it not only recognizes this subset of customer, but also explicitly models the degree of attrition to depend on customer attributes. Identification of this group of customers is crucial to any consumer finance business, since it provides the basis of efficient retention tactics and profitable target population. The chapter successfully demonstrates the improvement achieved by the double hurdle model over the conventional logistic regression technique in all the segments of attrition (over the different degrees of attrition).

3.1 Introduction

As an example of second generation model, this chapter introduces a class of models known as Double Hurdle Models (originally proposed by Cragg (1971)), which allows the potential attrition and the extent of attrition to be modeled separately. We develop an attrition model using a double hurdle model for a European auto portfolio. The chapter is organized as follows: Sect. 5.2 gives a brief literature on double hurdle model and discusses the methodology proposed in this chapter. Section 5.3 narrates the description of the data used. Section 5.4 provides the results. Section 5.5 compares the results of the double hurdle model with the conventional attrition model based on logistic regression. Finally, the conclusions are provided in Sect. 5.6.

This chapter contains contributions from S. Raja Sethu Durai, Madras School of Economics, Chennai, India.

S.N. Bhaduri and D. Fogarty, *Advanced Business Analytics*,
DOI 10.1007/978-981-10-0727-9_3

3.2 Double Hurdle Model

While examining the demand for durable goods, Cragg (1971) argued that in some situations the decision to acquire a durable good and the amount of acquisition is not always intimately related. Acquisition will occur only when desired acquisition is positive, but for any real acquisition two hurdles have to be crossed: First a positive amount has to be desired and second a favorable situation has to be there to implement that positive desire by actual acquisition. Number of studies have followed suit by using this double hurdle model in various aspects from estimating cigarette consumption (Jones 1989) to wild life valuation (Espineira 2004). On the credit scoring front Dionne et al. (1996) argued that estimating the default probabilities is not sufficient for appropriate evaluation of credit scoring and proposed a similar model. Moffat (2005) used a double hurdle model to estimate loan default.

3.2.1 *Methodology*

Before we describe the double hurdle model, it may be useful to start with a simple Tobit Model.

3.2.2 *Tobit*

First, consider a linear specification:

$$y_i^* = x_i'\beta + u_i \qquad i = 1, \Lambda, n$$

$$u_i \sim N(0, \sigma^2) \tag{3.1}$$

where y_i^* is a latent variable representing the borrower i's propensity to attrite, x_i is a vector of a borrower characteristics relevant in explaining the extent of attrition, β is a corresponding vector of parameters to be estimated, and u_i is a homoscedastic, normally distributed error term. Let y_i be the extent of attrition (e.g. loan term left > 0).[1] Since loan term left cannot be negative, the relationship between y_i^* and y_i is:

$$y_i = \max(y_i^*, 0) \tag{3.2}$$

Equation (3.2) gives rise to the standard censored regression model widely known as Tobit model. The log-likelihood function for the Tobit model is given as:

[1]Note loan term left = 0 implies not an attrition.

$$\text{Log}\, L = \sum_{0} \text{In}\left[1 - \Phi\left(\frac{x_i'\beta}{\sigma}\right)\right] + \sum_{+} \text{In}\left[\frac{1}{\sigma}\phi\left(\frac{y_i - x_i'\beta}{\sigma}\right)\right] \tag{3.3}$$

in which "0" indicates summation over the zero observations in the sample, while "+" indicates summation over positive observations. $\Phi(.)$ and ϕ (.) are the standard normal cdf and pdf respectively.

3.2.3 Double Hurdle Model

As the name suggests, a consumer in a double hurdle framework must cross two hurdles in order to attrite. The "first hurdle" needs to be crossed in order to be a potential attritor. Given that the borrower is a potential attritor, their current circumstances then dictate whether or not they do in fact attrite—the "second hurdle".

The double hurdle model contains two equations. We write:

$$d_i^* = z_i'\alpha + \varepsilon_i$$

$$y_i^{**} = x_i'\beta + u_i$$

$$\begin{pmatrix} \varepsilon_i \\ u_i \end{pmatrix} \sim N\left[\begin{pmatrix} 0 \\ 0 \end{pmatrix}, \begin{pmatrix} 1 \\ 0 \end{pmatrix}\right] \tag{3.4}$$

Note from the diagonality of the covariance matrix that the two error terms are assumed to be independently distributed.

The first hurdle is then represented by:

$d_i = 1$ if $d_i^* \geq 0$

$$d_i = 0$$

$$\text{If } d_i^* \leq 0 \tag{3.5}$$

Equation (3.5) is, therefore close to a Probit representation. The second hurdle closely resembles the Tobit model (3.2):

$$y_i^* = \max\left(y_i^{**}, 0\right) \tag{3.6}$$

Finally, the observed variable y_i, is determined as:

$$y_i = d_i y_i^* \tag{3.7}$$

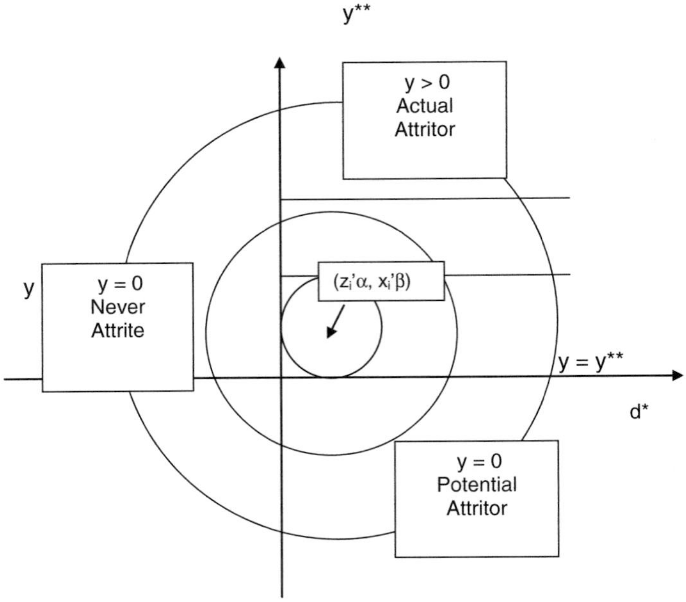

Fig. 3.1 The relationship between latent (d^* and y^{**}) variable and observed variable in double hurdle model. *Source* Moffat (2005)

The log-likelihood function for the double hurdle is:

$$\text{Log}\, L = \sum_0 \text{In}\left[1 - \Phi(z_i'\alpha)\Phi\left(\frac{x_i'\beta}{\sigma}\right)\right] + \sum_+ \text{In}\left[\Phi(z_i'\alpha)\frac{1}{\sigma}\phi\left(\frac{y_i - x_i'\beta}{\sigma}\right)\right] \quad (3.8)$$

A diagram below may be useful for understanding the model defined in (3.5)–(3.8). The Maximum likelihood estimation is applied to estimate α and β jointly along with the σ (Fig. 3.1).

3.2.4 *Prediction*

Estimating the predicted values of d_i and y_i* are as important as estimating the α, β. The predictions are constructed in two steps as follows: From the estimated α coefficient the probability of attrition is calculated as $\hat{p}(\text{attrition}) = \Phi(z_i'\alpha)$ which is similar to that of a Probit probability of attrition. The extent of attrition is then calculated as $\hat{y}_i = \Phi(x_i'\beta/\sigma) * \left\{x_i'\beta + \sigma * \left(\frac{\phi(x_i'\beta/\sigma)}{\Phi(x_i'\beta/\sigma)}\right)\right\}$

Finally, the expected loan term covered is given as: $\hat{p}(\text{attrition}) * \hat{y}_i$.

3.2.5 Estimation

There is no standard routine available in SAS to estimate a double hurdle model. One needs to write a program using Maximum Likelihood routine PROC NLMIXED available in SAS.

3.3 Data

Auto loan data of a European finance business have been used in this study. Total number of observation is 157,939 of which terminated accounts are 74,633. We considered only the terminated accounts to build the double hurdle model. Out of 74,633 terminated accounts, we further split it into 70:30 as development and validation sample. Final set of development sample has 52,243 observations and the validation sample with 22,390 observations. A careful look into the terminated accounts will reveal two interesting facts that 80 % of total loan lend out are 37–72 months term loans and 79 % of clients tend to pay back the loan after 2 years but

Table 3.1 Total amount financed and contractual term of the loan

Contractual term	Total amount financed	
	Sum	*N*
Contractual term $\leq$ 12	6,587,833	3206
12 < contractual term $\leq$ 24	33,432,392	6878
24 < contractual term $\leq$ 36	105,780,870	12,984
36 < contractual term $\leq$ 48	159,518,635	17,732
48 < contractual term $\leq$ 60	344,918,317	29,685
60 < contractual term $\leq$ 72	141,772,334	13,080
72 < contractual term $\leq$ 84	15,834,364	2987
84 < contractual term $\leq$ 96	76,221	1990
96 < contractual term $\leq$ 108	1987	1987

Table 3.2 Month on book (MOB) of the terminated accounts

MOB term	*N*
MOB_Term $\leq$ 12	8282
12 < MOB_Term $\leq$ 24	11,022
24 < MOB_Term $\leq$ 36	15,376
36 < MOB_Term $\leq$ 48	16,168
48 < MOB_Term $\leq$ 60	17,666
60 < MOB_Term $\leq$ 72	5241
72 < MOB_Term $\leq$ 84	258
84 < MOB_Term $\leq$ 96	211
96 < MOB_Term $\leq$ 108	201
MOB_Term > 108	201

Table 3.3 Terminated accounts and the loan term covered

LTC	Frequency	Percent	Cumulative freq	Cumulative percent
LTC < 0.25	7699	10.46	7501	10.21
0.25 ≤ LTC < 0.50	7757	10.53	15,258	20.78
0.50 ≤ LTC < 0.75	7886	10.71	23,144	31.52
0.75 ≤ LTC < 1	6190	8.41	29,334	39.94
LTC ≥ 1	44,104	59.89	73,438	100.0

before 6 years. Table 3.1 provides contractual term with the total amount financed. Table 3.2 gives an account of Month on Book (MOB) of the terminated accounts.

The Loan Term Covered (LTC) at the point of termination also depicts a similar picture of around 40 % of accounts are closed before covering the contractual term with 31 % is closed before LTC less than 75 %. Table 3.3 gives the number of accounts closed against the LTC covered. These numbers clearly indicate that the early termination is a big concern to worry and an effective strategy to identify the early termination will hold the key to prevent it through customized strategies.

3.3.1 *Variables Used*

The study uses all the terminated accounts as of Dec 2004. The data consists of accounts opened from 1993 to Dec 2004. An early termination flag has been created. The flag takes the value of 1 if the accounts are terminated before the actual loan term and 0 otherwise. Also we compute two additional variables namely Loan Term Covered (LTC) and Loan Term Left (LTL) as follows: For the accounts that have been terminated before completing the actual loan term the LTC is defined as LTC = (MOB till the time of termination)/Actual Loan Term. For all the other accounts, it is defined as LTC = 1. The LTL is calculated as (1 − LTC).

The selections of independent variables in the model are carried out after checking for correlation and multi-colinearity. Finally, two robustness checks have been performed for the proposed model: First, the model is developed for the development sample and the results have been validated for the validation sample. Second, an out of sample validation for all the accounts opened between January 1998 and December 2000 has been performed.

3.4 Results

The estimates of the double hurdle model proposed in this chapter are reported in Table 3.4. The sample size used in the estimation is 52,843. All the variables included in the model are significant at 99.99 % level. Selection of variables is done through a routine multi-collinearity check, having all VIFs less than 1.75. Focusing

Table 3.4 Double Hurdle model estimates

Variable	Definition	Coefficient	SE	*t*-value	*P* value
First hurdle					
Intercept		−0.12987	0.00834	−15.58	<0.0001
d2_NUMER	24 < no of Installments ≤ 36	−0.31998	0.00705	−45.45	<0.0001
d3_NUMER	36 < no of Installments ≤ 48	−0.16995	0.00615	−27.62	<0.0001
d5_NUMER	No of installments > 60	0.15663	0.00753	20.84	<0.0001
d1_limit	Credit limit = 0	−0.05706	0.01008	−5.66	<0.0001
d4_limit	Credit limit > 11419	0.04872	0.00765	6.37	<0.0001
d2_prime	4.9 < prime rate ≤ 5.6	0.18585	0.00531	35.07	<0.0001
d2_age	Age ≤ 34	0.07755	0.00618	12.53	<0.0001
d4_age	Age > 43	−0.07857	0.00609	−12.92	<0.0001
d5_margi	Margin > 3.1	0.07221	0.00597	12.1	<0.0001
d3_salar	Salary > 0.0491	0.039	0.00609	6.39	<0.0001
d1_TIPO_	Type of housing = 1	0.03909	0.00675	5.8	<0.0001
d2_TIPO_	Type of housing = 2	0.09816	0.00645	15.21	<0.0001
d4_TIPO_	Type of housing = 5	0.05985	0.01173	5.1	<0.0001
d1_TIN	Interest rate ≤ 7.5	−0.04734	0.0057	−8.29	<0.0001
d4_VALORE	Value of good > 16889	0.03	0.00522	5.75	<0.0001
d2_NUM_H	0 < number of children ≤ 1	0.03264	0.00861	3.8	0.0001
d3_ESTAD	Marital status = 3,4,5,6	0.03141	0.01059	2.96	0.003
d1_CARGO	Position of business = 1,2	0.0288	0.0051	5.65	<0.0001
d3_PRODU	Product code = 4–18	0.28269	0.01266	22.35	<0.0001
Sigma		0.08712	0.0006	147.2	<0.0001
Second hurdle					
Intercept		0.10062	0.00237	42.32	<0.0001
D1_NUMER	No of installments ≤ 24	−0.18261	0.00273	−66.89	<0.0001
D2_NUMER	24 < no of installments ≤ 36	−0.01227	0.00285	−4.32	<0.0001
D3_NUMER	36 < no of installments ≤ 48	−0.01839	0.00195	−9.46	<0.0001
D1_limit	Credit limit = 0	−0.09888	0.0036	−27.39	<0.0001
D2_prime	4.9 < prime rate ≤ 5.6	0.03207	0.00171	18.74	<0.0001
D2_age	Age <=34	0.00828	0.00147	5.6	<0.0001
D2_margi	1.65 < margin ≤ 2.1	−0.01446	0.00249	−5.84	<0.0001
D4_margi	2.65 < margin ≤ 3.1	0.00642	0.00204	3.15	0.0016
D5_margi	Margin > 3.1	0.00795	0.00177	4.45	<0.0001
D3_salar	Salary > 0.0491	0.01812	0.00165	11.01	<0.0001
D2_TIPO_	Type of housing = 2	0.01209	0.0015	8.07	<0.0001
D4_VALORE	Value of good > 16889	0.01722	0.00141	12.3	<0.0001
D2_NUM_H	0 < number of children ≤ 1	0.01164	0.00225	5.2	<0.0001
D3_ESTAD	Marital status = 3, 4, 5, 6	0.01068	0.00276	3.89	0.0001
D1_CARGO	Position of business = 1, 2	−0.00375	0.00141	−2.62	0.0088
D3_PRODU	Product code = 4–18	0.07053	0.00204	34.75	<0.0001

Note Any further description of the independent variables can't be provided due to the confidentiality agreement with data provider on the explanatory variables, numbers of installment, limit, prime rate, interest rate, value of the goods bought and product types seem to influence the first hurdle. Also a set of demographic variables such as age, marital status, type of housing, occupation has a strong influence on the first hurdle. It is interesting to note that the second hurdle is influenced by a different set of explanatory variables (different dummies), thereby justifying our choice of double hurdle model.

Since there is no standard goodness of fit measure available for the double hurdle model, we developed two criteria to validate our model: (a) Based on the predicted LTL, we check the Rank Order for three discrete segments: EEA (Early-Early Attrition with LTL > 0.75), EA (Early Attrition with LTL as $0.5 \leq \text{LTL} \leq 0.75$) and NEA (Not Early Attrition with LTL < 0.5). (b) Use a more direct method to calculate the prediction error using a cross-tab between the predicted EEA, EA and NEA and the actual segments. The rank–order data are reported in Tables 3.5 and 3.6. The estimated model rank-orders perfectly in all three segments for both the development and validation samples. The derived lift curve for the EEA is shown in Fig. 3.2. The KS is 54.1 for EEA, indicating a good fit.

Table 3.5 Development sample-decile for predicted LTL

Frequency	EEA	EA	NEA	Total
1	2127	1594	1421	5142
2	1079	1411	2653	5143
3	697	938	3507	5142
4	416	546	4181	5143
5	274	436	4433	5143
6	178	381	4583	5142
7	125	211	4807	5143
8	67	141	4934	5142
9	61	93	4989	5143
10	39	49	5055	5143
Total	4892	5629	40392	50913

Table 3.6 Validation sample-decile for predicted LTL

Frequency	EEA	EA	NEA	Total
1	905	746	585	2236
2	474	582	1180	2236
3	288	400	1548	2236
4	198	259	1779	2236
5	125	198	1913	2236
6	79	145	2012	2236
7	62	94	2080	2236
8	46	72	2118	2236
9	33	49	2154	2236
10	25	30	2181	2236
Total	2235	2575	17550	22360

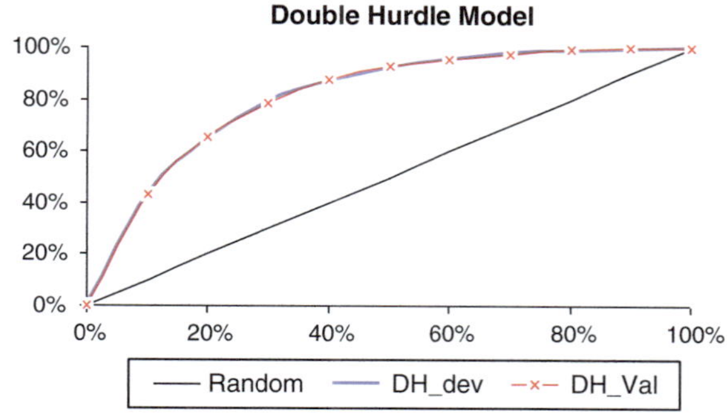

Fig. 3.2 Derived lift curve of the double hurdle model

Table 3.7 DH model—development sample with adjusted cut-off

	Predicted LTL			
	EEA	EA	NEA	Total
Actual LTL				
EEA	*2075*	1185	1670	4930
EA	1552	*1513*	2602	5667
NEA	1357	2918	*36155*	40430
Total	4984	5616	40427	51027

Note 78 % Correct prediction

Table 3.8 DH model—validation sample with adjusted cut-off

	Predicted LTL			
	EEA	EA	NEA	Total
Actual LTL				
EEA	*652*	694	1096	2442
EA	521	*867*	714	2102
NEA	1266	541	*15610*	17417
Total	2439	2102	17420	21961

Note 78.3 % Correct prediction

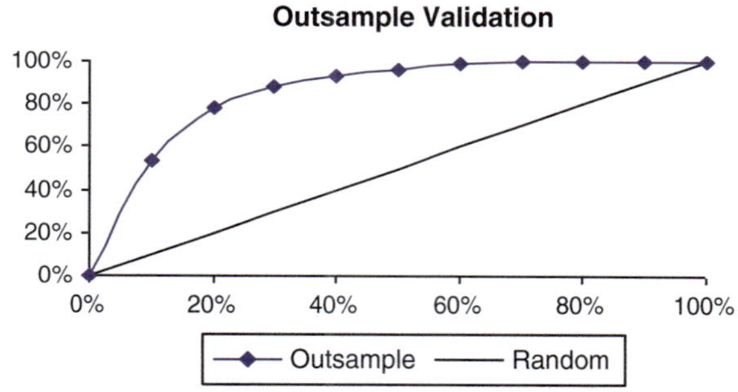

Fig. 3.3 The lift curve of the early early attrition

Table 3.9 DH model—out of sample validation

	Predicted LTL			
	EEA	EA	NEA	Total
Actual LTL				
Not EEA	0	23	*201*	224
Not EA	0	0	*79*	79
Total	0	23	261	284

The second goodness of fit measure based on the error of predictions is reported in Tables 3.7 and 3.8. In this case the predicted segments (EEA, EA, NEA) are defined based on a cut-off such that the proportions of these segments in the predicted population remains same as the actual population. The model predicts correctly in 78 % cases for both in development and validation sample.

Finally, we use an out of sample validation to assess the goodness of fit of our model. For the validation we consider all accounts opened between 1998 and 2000. The number of observations in the out of sample is 55,341 of which 49,024 are terminated accounts and 6515 are live accounts. The lift curve for EEA is presented in Fig. 3.3. The validation offers a perfect rank order for all three segments. For active accounts, we classify an account as "Not EEA" if it has already crossed less than 75 % of the LTL. The model correctly predicts 97 % cases as NEA indicating that the model validates quite well for the out sample as well. The results are in Table 3.9.

3.5 Beyond Logistic Regression

The received wisdom of developing an attrition model is to estimate the probability of early attrition using a logistic regression technique. Since we are also interested in identifying the extent of early attrition, we developed a double hurdle model in which the early attrition probability is estimated using a Probit model and Loan Term Left have been estimated using a Tobit model.

This section compares the strategy of using a conventional attrition model with a double hurdle model proposed in this chapter to exactly recognize the additional improvement achieved by double hurdle model over the traditional logistic regression. To make a successful comparison we adopt a three-step strategy: (a) we build an attrition model using a conventional logistic regression. The estimates of early attrition model are reported in Table 3.10. (b) Develop a strategy based on the logistics model: Select only top two deciles. (c) Compare the result with a double hurdle strategy.

As we select the customer in top two deciles using a conventional attrition model, the ex-post distribution of these accounts based on LTL is reported in Table 3.11. Despite its richness in capturing EEA, the conventional model wrongly targets 4544 (45 %) accounts, as they finally turned out to be NA (never attrite). Also the conventional method does not distinguish between EE and EA and hence cannot support a differential strategy based on the cost of attrition (e.g. loan term left). The primary

Table 3.10 Logistic regression results for development sample

Variable	Definition	Coefficient	SE	Chi-Sq	P value
Intercept		−1.22903	0.0382	1068.0729	<0.0001
d2_NUMER	24 < no of installments $\leq$ 36	−1.22293	0.0350	1257.5958	<0.0001
d3_NUMER	36 < no of installments $\leq$ 48	−0.49923	0.0281	342.0251	<0.0001
d5_NUMER	No of installments > 60	1.13187	0.0351	1006.2134	<0.0001
d1_limit	Limit = 0	−0.77563	0.0310	657.5039	<0.0001
d4_limit	Limit > 11419	0.42087	0.0369	118.1600	<0.0001
d2_prime	4.9 < prime rate $\leq$ 5.6	0.86567	0.0235	1299.0058	<0.0001
d2_age	Age $\leq$ 34	0.45107	0.0278	241.2134	<0.0001
d4_age	Age > 43	−0.37803	0.0293	184.8059	<0.0001
d5_margi	Margin > 3.1	0.33497	0.0268	138.0406	<0.0001
d3_salar	Salary > 0.0491	0.24607	0.0285	62.9291	<0.0001
d1_TIPO_	Type of housing = 1	0.23977	0.0323	46.4206	<0.0001
d2_TIPO_	Type of housing = 2	0.63477	0.0298	426.4740	<0.0001
d4_TIPO_	Type of housing = 5	0.31447	0.0543	29.4640	<0.0001
d1_TIN	Interest rate $\leq$ 7.5	−0.16333	0.0271	45.8513	<0.0001
d4_VALORE	Value of good > 16889	0.28967	0.0240	126.2166	<0.0001
d2_NUM_H	0 < number of children $\leq$ 1	0.24537	0.0400	31.7579	<0.0001
d3_ESTAD	Marital status = 3, 4, 5, 6	0.26547	0.0494	24.7360	<0.0001
d1_CARGO	Position of business = 1, 2	0.13387	0.0234	23.6397	<0.0001
d3_PRODU	Product code = 4–18	1.65087	0.0632	665.0305	<0.0001
Percent concordant	79.5	Somers'D	0.593		
Percent discordant	20.2	Gamma	0.595		
Percent tied	0.3	Tau-a	0.284		
Pairs	618630815	c	0.797		

Note Any further description of the independent variables can't be provided due to the confidentiality agreement with data provider

Table 3.11 Conventional attrition model (logistic regression), development sample

Top 2 decile				
	EEA	EA	NA	
Decile 1	2240	1714	1725	5679
Decile 2	1150	1315	3215	5680
	3390	3029	4940	11359
Total	5071	5808	40571	
Percentage	67 %	52 %	12 %	

Table 3.12 Decile for EEA—development sample

Frequency	EEA	EA	NEA	Total
1	323	194	32	549
2	301	208	41	550
3	320	178	52	550
4	289	133	127	549
5	195	151	204	550
6	182	172	196	550
7	164	173	212	549
8	157	176	217	550
9	152	170	228	550
10	163	168	219	550
Total	2246	1723	1528	5497

Table 3.13 Decile for EA—development sample

Frequency	EEA	EA	NEA	Total
1	170	185	257	612
2	148	200	265	613
3	135	196	282	613
4	137	170	306	613
5	146	158	309	613
6	129	155	329	613
7	124	176	313	613
8	145	158	310	613
9	101	166	346	613
10	121	120	372	613
Total	1356	1684	3089	6129

Table 3.14 Double Hurdle model, development sample

Double Hurdle model				
	EEA	EA	NEA	
Target customer base	3318	3124	4082	10524
Percentage	65.90 %	54.10 %	11.50 %	
Improvement	6.10 %	13.00 %	−12.60 %	

claim of the double hurdle model is not only to save potential NA customers, but also to offer a differential strategy for EEA and EA. As the double hurdle model predicts LTL we have segregated the target sample based on predicted EEA, EA and NEA. The distribution of customers in EEA and EA segments are given in Tables 3.12 and 3.13. Since our objective is to select a similar target base as used in the conventional approach, we have decided to select all deciles in EEA and top nine deciles in EA segments. This has left us with a target of 9930 customers.

Table 3.15 Double Hurdle model, validation sample

Logistic regression				
Top 2 decile				
	EEA	EA	NEA	
Decile 1	1062	878	833	2773
Decile 2	581	680	1512	2773
	1643	1558	2345	5546
Total	2243	2385	17360	
Percentage	73 %	65 %	14 %	
Double Hurdle model				
	EEA	EA	NEA	
Target customer base	1504	1454	1824	4782
Percentage	65.80 %	54.60 %	11.30 %	
Improvement	6.60 %	10.00 %	−14.70 %	

The ex-post distribution of the accounts targeted though the double hurdle model is reported in Table 3.14. The following table clearly demonstrates the success of the double hurdle model over the conventional attrition model. This has not only improved the prediction power of EEA by 4.2 % and EA by 11.1 %, but also saved an additional 14.5 % in the NEA segment. We carry out a similar exercise for the holdout sample and the results are reported in Table 3.15. The validation corroborates a similar success of the double hurdle model over the conventional approach.

3.6 Conclusion

The chapter develops a double hurdle model that challenges the conventional wisdom of building an attrition model using a logistic regression technique. The methodology developed in this chapter clearly recognizes the existence of a group of potential attritor who would never attrite under any circumstances. Most importantly, the double hurdle model not only recognizes existence of this group of customer but also explicitly models the probability of actual attrition to depend on customer attributes. Finally, the model successfully demonstrates the improvement over the conventional technique in all segments of attrition, EEA, EA and NEA.

References

Cragg JG (1971) Some statistical models for limited dependent variables with application to the demand for durable goods. Econometrica 39(5):829–844

Dionne G, Artis M, Guillen M (1996) Count data models for a credit scoring system. J Empir Finance 3(3):303–325
Espineira RM (2004) A box-cox double-hurdle model of wildlife valuation: the citizen's perspective. In: Chapter presented on the Sixth Annual BIOECON Conference held at Kings College Cambridge, 2–3 September 2004
Jones A (1989) A double-hurdle model of cigarette consumption. J Appl Econ 4(1):23–39
Moffat P (2005) Hurdle models of loan default. J Oper Res Soc 56:1063–1071

Chapter 4
Optimizing the Media Mix—Evaluating the Impact of Advertisement Expenditures of Different Media

Saumitra N. Bhaduri, S. Raja Sethu Durai and David Fogarty

Abstract Focusing on the consumer finance business of a large financial company of Europe, this chapter analyzes the efficiency of advertising expenditures on three media—TV, print, and the Internet. Using a data envelopment analysis (DEA) method, it assesses the overall efficiency of the media and the effective combinations in attracting new loan applications. It develops an optimal media mix model to evaluate the effect of different media expenditure in getting the approved new loans to the business. Total cost per week for TV, print, and Internet is used as inputs and two outputs; namely, approved new loans and calls received per week are used within a DEA framework to estimate the efficiency score. The incremental benefits from this analysis were estimated at 38 %. The efficiency score developed in this chapter clearly recognizes the best practices weeks, with that we can identify the best combination of media, which serves the purpose best in terms of acquiring new loan applications. Finally, a media mix builder is developed to guide the business for the future strategies. Advertising analytics is gaining momentum as a powerful means to efficient targeting. Sir Martin Sorell, CEO of WPP Group, one of the world's largest advertising agencies, calls econometrics the holy grail of advertising. Moreover, several top advertising agencies have now created teams of econometricians to do this type of analysis for clients. Therefore, this research and further research in this area are necessary to insure that advertising resources are well spent.

This chapter contains contributions from S. Raja Sethu Durai, Madras School of Economics, Chennai, India.

S.N. Bhaduri and D. Fogarty, *Advanced Business Analytics*,
DOI 10.1007/978-981-10-0727-9_4

4.1 Introduction

John Wanamaker, founder of the first department store and considered to be the father of modern advertising once, stated "Half the money I spend on advertising is wasted: the trouble is, I don't know which half." The theoretical expectations of advertising practice are not fully satisfied in reality. High level of advertising inefficiency has been recognized and documented in the marketing literature by many studies. Bass (1979) observed that much of the advertising spending is wasted and the level of waste for some companies could reach as high as 407 % of their net income. Since large sum of money is spent on advertising, these documented inefficiencies are a cause of worry for all the practitioners and the business.

Since the 1960s, there have been a few efforts by the research community to empirically evaluate the efficiency of advertising and to suggest ways to increase that efficiency. In 1978, Charnes, Cooper, and Rhodes developed data envelopment analysis (DEA), a nonparametric methodology for benchmarking efficiency. Luo and Donthu (2001) are the first to use the DEA in analyzing the efficiency of advertising expenditures. The advertising industry will continue to be revolutionized by quantitative analyses. In the past, many firms assumed that the world of advertising and branding was an art and did not apply much scientific rigor in measuring the effectiveness of this marketing activity. The reason for this is probably historical due to the creative aspects of formulating messages and the very difficult task of measuring and quantifying human behavior. Today, however, the use of quantitative methods to analyze the efficiency of advertising expenditures is becoming increasingly important to firms as global competition is forcing them to prioritize their advertising budgets on a worldwide basis. Moreover, the Web channel is increasingly taking a higher percentage of advertising spent as demonstrated in Google's recent success in significantly growing its revenues and profits. The Web channel also provides an easier way to track the effectiveness of each advertising message (Davenport and Harris 2007).

Using weekly data on the advertising expenditure of a business, this chapter identifies the best practice weeks using DEA method. This chapter is organized as follows: Sect. 4.2 gives a brief literature review on efficiency measurements with its two procedures and the DEA methodology. Section 4.3 narrates the description of the data used. Section 4.4 provides the results. Finally Sect. 4.5 provides the conclusion.

4.2 Efficiency Measurement

Modern efficiency measurement begins with Farrell (1957) who drew upon the work of Debreu (1951) and Koopmans (1951) to define a simple measure of efficiency, which could account for multiple inputs. He theorized that a firm efficiency consists of two components: technical efficiency, which reflects the ability of a firm

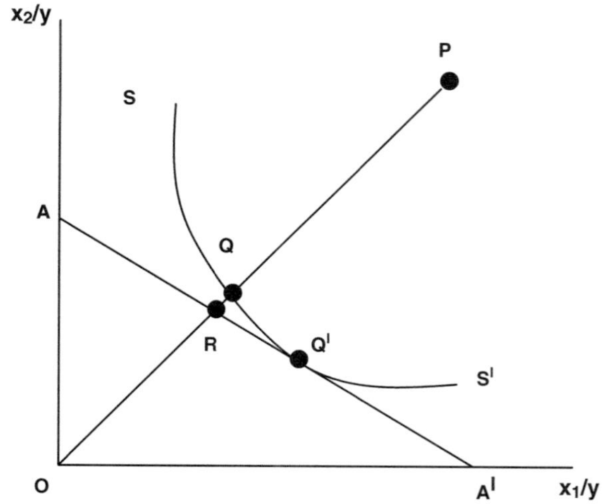

Fig. 4.1 Input-oriented measure of technical efficiency and allocative efficiency

to obtain maximum output with a given set of inputs, and allocative efficiency, which reflects the ability of a firm to use the inputs in optimal proportions, given their respective prices. The product of these two measures provides the total economic efficiency of a firm.

Following Farrell (1957), two different measures are gained prominence in the efficiency measurement literature, namely the input-oriented measure and the output-oriented measure.

4.2.1 Input-Oriented Measures

A simple example is illustrated in Fig. 4.1. Consider a firm that uses two inputs (x_1 and x_2) to produce one output (y). Under the assumption of constant returns to scale, SSl curve represents the efficient isoquant. If a firm uses quantities of inputs defined by the point P, to produce a unit output, the distance QP defines the technical inefficiency of the firm, since the Q is technically efficient because it lies in the efficient isoquant. So technical efficiency TEI = OQ/OP. The TEI takes the value between zero and one and gives the degree of technical inefficiency. A value of one indicates the firm is fully technically efficient.

If the input price ratio, represented by the line AAl, is known, then the allocative efficiency of the firm operating at the point P is AEI = OR/OQ. Since Q is technically efficient and allocative inefficient point. The distance RQ represents the production costs that should be reduced to push it to the efficient point Q_I.

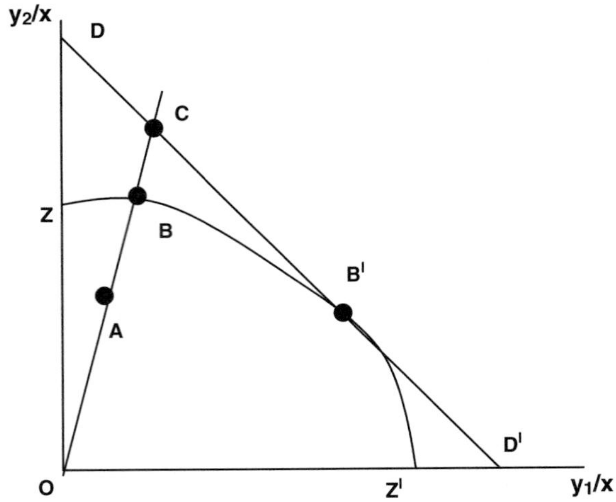

Fig. 4.2 Output-oriented measure of technical efficiency and allocative efficiency

4.2.2 Output-Oriented Measures

The input-oriented measure addresses the question: "By how much can the input quantities be proportionally reduced without changing the output produced?" Instead, we can also ask, "by how much can the output quantities be proportionally expanded without changing the inputs used?" This provides us the output-oriented measure. An example is illustrated in Fig. 4.2.

Consider a firm that produces two outputs (y_1 and y_2) with one input (x). In Fig. 4.2, the line ZZl represents the production possibility curve. A firm operation at point *A* is an inefficient firm. Here, the distance AB is technical inefficiency of the firm, since the point B lies in the production possibility curve. The technical efficiency TEo = OA/OB. If we have the price information, we can construct the isorevenue curve DDl and define the allocative efficiency as follows

$$\mathrm{AEo} = \mathrm{OB}/\mathrm{OC}$$

To bridge the distance BC, the inputs have to be increased to attain allocation efficiency.

4.2.3 Date Envelopment Analysis

Data envelopment analysis (DEA) is a nonparametric mathematical programming approach to evaluate the relative efficiency of comparable firms. Charnes et al. (1978) introduced a DEA model, which formed the basis for all subsequent developments in DEA and called as CCR model. The CCR model introduced the generic term "decision making units" (DMUs) to describe the collection of units which have common inputs and outputs and which are being assessed for efficiency. The CCR had an input orientation and assumed constant returns to scale (CRS). Subsequently, the CRS assumption is only suitable if all the DMUs in question operate at an optimal scale. But imperfect competition and other operating constraints force the DMUs to operate in a variable returns to scale. Banker et al. (1984) proposed a variable returns to scale (VRS) model. Both output-orientated and input-orientated models are very similar dual problems. The generic input-orientated model is as follows:

$$\begin{aligned}
&\min \theta - \varepsilon\left(\sum_{i=1}^{m} s_i^- + \sum_{r=1}^{s} s_r^+\right)\\
&\sum_{j=1}^{n} \lambda_j x_{ij} + s_i^- = \theta\, x_{ijo} \quad i = 1, 2, \ldots, m\\
&\sum_{j=1}^{n} \lambda_j y_{rj} - s_r^+ = y_{rjo} \quad r = 1, 2, \ldots, s\\
&\sum_{j=1}^{n} \lambda_j = 1 \quad \lambda_j \geq 0 \quad j = 1, 2, \ldots, n
\end{aligned} \tag{4.1}$$

where DMU*jo* represents one of the *n* DMUs under evaluation, and x_{ijo} and y_{rjo} are the *i*th input and *r*th output for DMUo, respectively, and si^- and sr^+ represent the *i*th input and *r*th output slacks. ε is non-Archimedean, which allows minimization over θ. By solving (4.1), we get optimal solutions θ^* and λ^*. If the efficiency score θ^* is equal to 1, then the DMU is operating at the efficient frontier and the input levels are optimal. If the score is less than 1, then the current input level is sub-optimal and it should reduce the current inputs to the level of its reference sets, represented by λ*. The output-orientated model is as follows

$$\max_{\phi,\lambda} \phi,$$

subject to

$$-\phi\, y_i + Y\lambda \geq 0,$$

$$x_i - X\lambda \geq 0,$$

$$N1'\lambda = 1,\ \lambda \geq 0$$

where $1 \leq \phi < \infty$, and $\phi - 1$ is the proportional increase in outputs that could be achieved by the *i*th DMU, with input quantities held constant. N1 is an N × 1 vector of ones. This convexity constraint $N1'\lambda = 1$ represents the scale; if it is included, then the model assumes variable returns to scale (VRS).

4.2.4 Estimation

There is no standard routine available in SAS to estimate this DEA model. There are plenty of freeware available in the Internet to do this DEA estimation. We used a freeware called DEAP 1.1 to estimate the weekly efficiency score.

4.3 Data

Scrambled data from a sample business have been used in this study. We considered the data on media expenditure for a typical financial services product. Weekly total cost on three different media, namely TV, Internet, and print, is considered as inputs, and approved new loans and calls received are considered as output. The data are available from first week of 2004 to twenty-sixth week of 2006. Totally 105 weeks are available for the analysis. The average cost per week in local currency for each media is given in Table 4.1. It clearly shows that the business spends more amount on TV, followed by print and then the new media Internet. Before going into the DEA analysis to estimate the efficiency score for each week, two preprocessing of the data is required to make each week comparable. First, the seasonal effect in the output data has to be normalized with deseasonalization. Second, the spillover effects of the media over the weeks are to be standardized.

4.3.1 Deseasonalization

A simple seasonal index is used to deseasonalize the data. The construction of the seasonal index for each week is as follows. First, calculate the average approved new loan applications for the entire time period. Second, take the ratio of the actual approved new loan application in a particular week and the average approved new loan applications. Third, the seasonal index for the first week of January is calculated as the average of the estimated ratios in the first week of January in 2004, 2005, and 2006. Further, dividing the actual approved new loan applications in a particular week with this seasonal index for that week will give the deseasonalized value. Figure 4.3 depicts the actual and deseasonalized data for the year 2004.

Table 4.1 Average cost per week

Media	Average cost			
	2004	2005	2006	Total
TV	193,132	334,306	474,290	308,546
print	149,778	112,358	197,381	136,361
Internet	29,073	45,527	62,339	43,113

Note Numbers are in local currencies

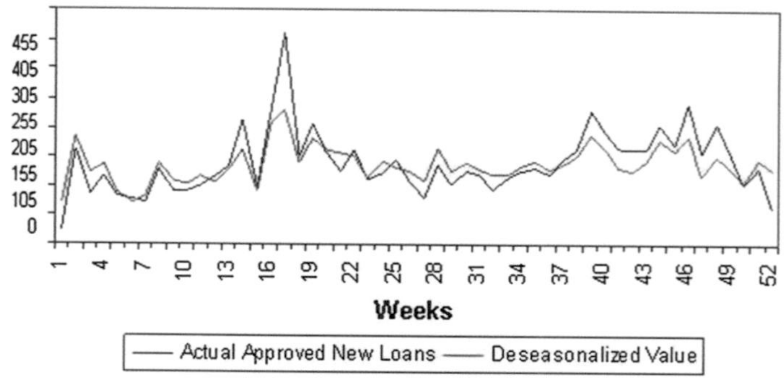

Fig. 4.3 Actual and deseasonalized output data for 2004

4.3.2 Adjusting Spillover Effects

An advertisement through a media or a combination of media in a particular week might have spillover effects in the following weeks in getting the new applications. In simple words, it means that an application in a particular week might not be a cause of the advertisements in that particular week, but it would be a reflection of the advertisements in the previous weeks. This spillover effect has to be adjusted to get an unbiased estimate of the efficiency score. To identify the spillover effect, a distributed lag regression model is used. The result of that model is given in Table 4.2 for the approved new loans and Table 4.3 for the calls received.

Table 4.2 Spillover effects on approved new loans

	Coefficients	Standard error	*T* stat	*P* value
Intercept	21.3712087	1.314688	16.256	0.000
TV	0.00001206	0.000004	3.315	0.001
Internet	0.00005006	0.000016	3.092	0.003
print	0.00001806	0.000006	3.226	0.002
TV(-1)	0.00001206	0.000004	3.386	0.001
print(-3)	0.00001806	0.000006	3.522	0.001
Regression statistics				
R square		0.451		
F statistics		15.818		
P value		0.000		
Observations		105		

Table 4.3 Spillover effects on calls received

	Coefficients	Standard error	*T* stat	*P* value
Intercept	242.639954	13.2728	18.282	0.000
print	0.00026	0.00006	3.791	0.000
print(-2)	0.0002	0.00006	2.871	0.005
Regression statistics				
R Square		0.232		
F Statistics		15.096		
P Value		0.000		
Observations		105		

4.3.3 *Model*

DEA output-orientated model with variable returns to scale is used in this weekly analysis of media expenditures. Efficient weeks, best practices, are those weeks in which no other combination of media expenditure can generate as much output in terms of approved new loans. The model is as follows:

$$\max \delta$$

$$\text{s.t} \sum \lambda_j (\text{TV})_j \geq (\text{TV})_{jo}$$

$$\text{s.t} \sum \lambda_j (\text{print})_j \geq (\text{print})_{jo}$$

$$\text{s.t} \sum \lambda_j (\text{Internet})_j \geq (\text{Internet})_{jo}$$

$$\delta (\text{Output})_{jo} \geq \sum \lambda_j (\text{Output})_j$$

$$\sum \lambda_j = 1$$

$$\lambda_j \geq 0, j = \text{weeks } 1, 2, \ldots, N$$

where δ = inefficiency parameter and λ = weights. In this model, the objective of the linear program is to maximize output production, with the given set of inputs.

4.4 Results

Total cost per week for three different media, namely TV, print, and Internet, is considered as input, and the seasonally adjusted data on approved new loans and calls received are used as output to estimate the efficiency score for each week using DEA methodology. Assuming variable returns to scale (VRS) and output orientation, the average efficiency score for all the 105 weeks is 0.888. Totally, 27 weeks are identified as best practices weeks with efficiency score of 1. In those 27, 14 weeks are identified in 2004, 6 weeks in 2005, and 7 weeks in 2006. Table 4 gives the number of times a particular combination of media appeared in the best practices week. Using all three media and the combination of Internet and print appears 6 times each out of 27 best practices weeks followed by only Internet appearing 5 times. The other combinations appear 3 times each except only TV that appears only one time. Using these best practices weeks and the estimated peers for each inefficient weeks, we validate the model in terms of incremental benefits in approved new loans and construct a media mix builder to effectively implement the model for future strategies. For validation, we regrouped the 105 weeks spanning across 3 years into 50 weeks starting from first week of January to third week of December.

Validation

The model validation has been done by calculating the incremental benefits in new approved loans. For each inefficient week, the DEA model has identified its peers. There is a possibility that the DEA can identify more than one peer. In that case, the peer having highest approved new loans has been considered as peer for that particular week. The incremental benefit is calculated as the difference between the actual seasonally adjusted approved new loans for a particular week and the seasonally adjusted approved new loans of its peer. For an efficient week, the peer is the week itself, so the incremental benefit is zero for efficient weeks. The total incremental benefit is calculated as 6179 seasonally adjusted approved new loans, which is 38 % of the actual adjusted approved new loans.

4.5 Conclusions

The chapter develops an optimal media mix model to evaluate the effect of different media expenditure in getting the approved new loans to the business. Weekly data on three inputs, namely the total cost per week for TV, print, and Internet, and two outputs, namely approved new loans and calls received per week, are used in a DEA framework to estimate the efficiency score along with the peers for each week. The results identified 27 weeks out of 105 weeks as efficient weeks. The incremental benefits are estimated at 38 %, which means that with the given inputs, the business can either improve the output or reduce the cost by 38 % with the given set of inputs and outputs, respectively. Finally, a media mix builder has been developed with the score and the peers' information for future strategies.

Sir Martin Sorell, CEO of WPP Group, one of the world's largest advertising agencies, calls econometrics the holy grail of advertising. Moreover, several top advertising agencies have now created teams of econometricians to do this type of analysis for clients. It is expected that firms will increasingly view analytics about advertising as a necessary adjunct to embarking upon any campaign (Davenport and Harris 2007). Therefore, this research and further research in this area is necessary to insure that advertising resources are well spent.

References

Banker R, Charnes A, Cooper W (1984) Some models for estimating technical and scale inefficiencies in data envelopment analysis. Manage Sci 30(9):1078–1092

Bass FM (1979) Advertising spending levels and promotion policies profit potential for the application of management science. Presented at the Eleventh Annual Albert Wesley Lecture, University of Pittsburgh

Charnes A, Cooper W, Rhodes E (1978) Measuring the efficiency of decision making units. Eur J Oper Res 3(6):429–444

Davenport TH, Harris JG (2007) Competing on analytics: The new science of winning, Harvard Business School Press

Debreu G (1951) The coefficient of resource utilization. Econometrica 19:273–292

Farrell MJ (1957) The measurement of productive efficiency. J R Stat Soc, Ser A 120(3):143–155

Koopmans TC (1951) Analysis of production as an efficient combination of activities. In: Koopmans (ed) Activity analysis of production and allocation proceedings of a conference, Cowles foundation monograph No 13

Luo X, Donthu N (2001) Benchmarking advertising efficiency. J Advertising Res 41(6):7–18

Chapter 5
Strategic Retail Marketing Using DGP-Based Models

Saumitra N. Bhaduri, V. Anuradha, S. Raja Sethu Durai and David Fogarty

Abstract Most retail businesses operate in a non-contractual settings, and this relationship with the customers poses difficulties in differentiating between the customers who have attrited voluntarily and those who are in the middle of their long cycle transaction behavior. Therefore, formulating an effective CRM strategy in retail poses a significant challenge. This chapter proposes a DGP (data generating process)-based predictive strategy with the past purchase transaction data, which would help the business to improve the overall marketing performance with minimum data requirement. In contrast to many existing RFM (recency, frequency, and monetary value)-based models, a set of model with strong underlying behavioral model is proposed, thereby providing a greater insight into the customer decisions. The approach basically predicts a customer's future purchase money value by combining the three key transaction factors, viz. recency, frequency, and monetary value which is further combined into a more powerful single predicted value (PRFM) for each customer. This represents an original contribution as many retailers are making decisions with RFM, but these are anchored on a static metric based on looking at past behavior and are not predictive in nature. Furthermore, when they do try to render RFM predictive, the methods are often ad hoc, and therefore, they are usually difficult to implement in practice. The final and most important characteristic of this model is the extensibility. Though the models depend only on three key customer attributes, R, F, and M, it can be easily extended to incorporate other customer attributes of interest by running the algorithm for each subsegment. Suggestions for future research include the adaptation of these techniques to all types of general-purpose revolving credit cards which are being issued by most banks and consumer finance companies.

This chapter contains contributions from S. Raja Sethu Durai, Madras School of Economics, Chennai, India.

S.N. Bhaduri and D. Fogarty, *Advanced Business Analytics*,
DOI 10.1007/978-981-10-0727-9_5

5.1 Introduction

Understanding the customers and serving their interest is the forte of effective CRM practice. In retail businesses, cash is a key tender item, and therefore, these firms often face a challenge in executing an effective CRM program since there is a lack of customer data available. Typically, retailers have a good understanding of what has been purchased and how much; however, they often do not understand who is making these purchases. This is a critical piece of knowledge to be able to launch an effective CRM program. Retailers have been able to mitigate this by deploying customer loyalty initiatives and launching successful retail credit programs which allow them to capture customer data. A retail credit program can consist of private-label credit cards, cobranded bankcards, prepaid debit cards, and closed-end sales finance loans. The primary goal of these programs is to drive incremental sales for the retailer and to provide an additional revenue stream from interest income. Another goal is to extract insights from the data from these products as a vehicle to execute CRM programs to increase retail sales and subsequent revolving balances on the card. Typically, this is accomplished by following traditional retail CRM practices. Tesco, the UK-based global retailer, is a leader in this area. Tesco, working with their database marketing partner Dunnhumby, has taken the data from their successful Clubcard loyalty product launch, has extracted detailed insights on customer's purchase behavior patterns, and has developed CRM programs which have been effective at driving incremental sales for the firm. Tesco has been so successful at creating loyal customers using this methodology that they have moved from being the 3rd most successful retailer in the UK to number one across a variety of KPI's post-CRM implementation. Other companies have begun to follow suit with the same model including Kroger which is a large supermarket chain in the USA. Catalina Marketing helps the grocery industry to understand the effect of coupons and other promotions through selling its analytical services. Every week, Catalina retrieves about 250 million transactions from more than 21,000 grocery stores. Catalina manages one of the largest databases in the world which contains the purchase histories of over 100 million households on behalf of those stores. The analytical approach used by Catalina is to aggregate information from their database about purchase behavior and customer demographics along with their attitudes and preferences. Catalina then sells these insights to grocery store chains and packaged goods companies. Catalina attests to the fact that its analytically based approach can increase a company's average coupon-redemption rates up to ten times higher than they would be with traditional promotion methods (Davenport and Harris 2007). In the retail business, two important aspects often emerge as primary concerns to be addressed: first, identification of the dormant customer, particularly those operating in a non-contractual setting as it poses difficulty in understanding whether a long hiatus of the customer is due to their long cycle transaction behavior or their terminated relationship with the business. Second, even if the business identifies the active customers, modeling their future transaction behavior can prove to be cumbersome with the plethora of choice of variables and the techniques available.

Therefore to understand the customer base and their future transaction behavior, Schmittlein et al. (1987) proposed a Pareto/NBD model based on two pieces of information from the past purchasing history such as the "recency" (i.e., information on when the last purchase happened) and the "frequency" (i.e., details on number of purchases happened in a particular time period). Using these two information, Schmittlein et al. (1987) derived the key statistics, namely the probability that a customer is still active and also the expected number of transaction in the next time period.

However, the NBD assumes that for any live customer, the transaction may happen at any point in time. Therefore, for purchase occurring in discrete-time intervals as in many retail businesses, it might not be appropriate to use Pareto/NBD model. To capture the discrete purchase behavior in retail business, Fader et al. (2004) proposed a beta-geometric/beta-binomial (BG/BB) model for such discrete-time analog cases. Similar to Pareto/NBD, BG/BB model also derives two key statistics such as the probability of active and expected number of purchases in the next time period.

The third and most important aspect of consumer behavior, i.e., the money value of the expected future purchases, is modeled following the models proposed by Fader et al. (2005).

The contribution of this chapter is threefold: First, since targeting the right customer has emerged as key objective to successful database marketing, a very common practice has been to use the RFM (recency, frequency, and monetary value) of past responses to estimate the likelihood of future behavior. At a high level, this technique allows retailers to separate the "cherry pickers" from their loyal regular customers. Consequently, a plethora of techniques ranging from simple regression to neural networks have been used to establish the relationship between RFM and response. Although these approaches remain the workhorse for the industry, they suffer from serious drawbacks. Despite the predictive successes and their familiarity as standard industry techniques, these RFM-based "top-down" approaches often fail to generate the explanatory insight into the customer behavior. It is important to recognize that this approach as a successful tool to identify explanatory variables in a customer response model often leads to correlates rather than identifying genuine drivers of customer behavior. Furthermore, most of the "top-down" approaches are designed to capture the average behavior, thereby ignoring the customer heterogeneity as noise. However as DeSarbo and Ramaswamy (1994) pointed out, the understanding of the nature of customer heterogeneity can serve as an important element for more accurate prediction as well as for creative marketing strategy. In contrast, the "bottom-up" approach proposed in this chapter is deeply rooted in the consumer behavior theory encompassing all the possible heterogeneous response behavior of the customers.

Second, retail analytics is often considered as a discipline of "pattern recognition." However with the introduction of advanced econometrics in retail analytics, the focus has shifted from modeling the "outcome" to the underlying "data generation process (DGP)." The DGP-based model proposed in this chapter develops a behavioral model that uses observation from the past responses to predict future behavior.

Finally, most of the "top-down" models heavily rely on the normality assumption, thereby force fitting the model into the observations. Don Schultz (1995) pointed out “The more we learn about customers and prospects, the less they fit into the normally distributed theory. In fact, in many categories and in many businesses, the curve isn’t normal at all. It’s inverted. It’s a U-shape or sometimes even a V-shape. …Technology is teaching us that they [customers] certainly don’t seem normally distributed in marketing. …What the academic community should be doing [is] challenging the status quo.” Therefore, following this tradition, the model proposed in this chapter does not assume normality as underlying customer attribute.

This chapter attempts to validate the proposed empirical model using the past purchasing data from three different retail businesses across the globe and corroborates the efficacy of the model in clearly segmenting customers on their activeness and value. This chapter organizes as follows: Sect. 5.2 gives a brief narration of the methodology. Section 5.3 describes the data. Section 5.4 presents the results and explains the construction of retail strategy booster, and the final Sect. 5.5 concludes with a summary.

5.2 Methodology

This chapter closely follows the methodology prescribed by Fader et al. (2004). A customer’s purchase transaction can be represented in binary terms as 1 for purchase and 0 for no purchase. A transaction stream is represented as (x, n, m) where x is the number of purchase occurred in n transaction opportunities with the last transaction happened at $m \leq n$. For example, reading from left to right, the purchase string 0 1 0 1 1 0 0 0 can be summarized as $(x = 3, n = 8, m = 5)$. Given this summary of purchase transaction behavior, the model tries to estimate the probability of activeness and expected number of transaction in a specific future time period. However, the model is complete from a business perspective only if the money value of future transaction is known. To estimate the average money value of future transaction, average money value across the x number of purchase is captured. Using only these four data information, this chapter estimates the following statistics. The probability that a customer is active in the next specified time period and his/her expected number of transaction with average money value is conditional on their past purchase transaction stream.

5.2.1 Model Likelihood Function

With the assumptions listed in Fader et al. (2004), this model is built on beta-binomial and beta-geometric distributions.[1] More generally for a customer

[1]For a detailed description on the assumptions and derivation of the likelihood function refer Fader et al. (2004).

with a purchase transaction history (x, n, m), the likelihood for probability of activeness p will be as follows:

$$L(p, q/x, n, m) = p^x(1-p)^{n-x}(1-q)^n + \sum_{i=0}^{n-m-1} p^x(1-p)^{m-x+i}q(1-q)^{m+i}$$

For a randomly chosen customer, an expectation of the above equation over the mixing distribution of p and q gives the following:

$$\begin{aligned} L(\alpha, \beta, \gamma, \delta/x, n, m) &= \int\int_0^1 L(p, q/x, n, m)f(p/\alpha, \beta)f(q/\gamma, \delta)\mathrm{d}p\mathrm{d}q \\ &= \frac{B(\alpha+x, \beta+n-x)}{B(\alpha, \beta)}\frac{B(\gamma, \delta+n)}{B(\gamma, \delta)} \\ &+ \sum_{i=0}^{n-m-1}\frac{B(\alpha+x, \beta+m-x+i)}{B(\alpha, \beta)}\frac{B(\gamma+1, \delta+m+i)}{B(\gamma, \delta)} \end{aligned}$$

The four model parameters (α, β, γ, δ) can be estimated by maximum likelihood method of the following sample likelihood function using standard numerical optimization tools.

$$\mathrm{LL}(\alpha, \beta, \gamma, \delta) = \sum_{i=1}^{N}\ln[L(\alpha, \beta, \gamma, \delta/x_i, n_i, m_i)]$$

where N is the sample size and ith customer's purchase transaction stream is denoted as (x_i, n_i, m_i).

5.2.2 Derivation of P(active|x, n, m)

For a customer with a purchase transaction history (x, n, m), the probability that he is active in the $n + 1$ period is given by:

$$P(\text{active}/x, n, m, p, q) = \frac{p^x(1-p)^{n-x}(1-q)^{n+1}}{L(p, q/x, n, m)}$$

Taking the expectation of the above equation over the mixing distribution of p and q, it can be generalized for a randomly chosen customer as follows:

$$P(\text{active}/x, n, m, \alpha, \beta, \gamma, \delta) = \frac{B(\alpha + x, \beta + n - x)}{B(\alpha, \beta)} \times \frac{B(\gamma, \delta + n + 1)}{B(\gamma, \delta)} / L(\alpha, \beta, \gamma, \delta / x, n, m)$$

5.2.3 *Expected Number of Future Transaction*

Let $E(X^* \mid n^*, x, n, m)$ denote the expected number of purchases over the next n^* periods by a customer with purchase transaction history (x, n, m). Assuming the customer is active at the beginning of period $n + 1$, the expected number of transaction in the next n^* transaction opportunities can be characterized and generalized for a randomly chosen customer by taking expectation of the joint posterior distribution of p and q.

$$E\,(X^*/n^*, x, n, m, \alpha, \beta, \gamma, \delta) = \frac{B\,(\alpha + x + 1, \beta + n - x)}{B(\alpha, \beta)} \times \left[\frac{B(\gamma - 1, \delta + n + 1) - B(\gamma - 1, \delta + n + n^* + 1)}{B(\gamma, \delta)}\right] / L(\alpha, \beta, \gamma, \delta / x, n, m)$$

5.2.4 *Average Money Value of Future Transaction*

Following Fader et al. (2005), the average money value of future transaction is modeled separately. It is important to address two basic issues before modeling the money value as a separate model. First, can the average money value based on the past transaction history be used to estimate the value of future transactions? Second, are the distribution of average transaction value same as the transaction process?

Unfortunately, the answers to this twin issue seem negative: First, the mean of an expenditure stream by a customer cannot be fully trusted as the true underlying average transaction value of that customer. Second, the correlation between average transaction value and number of transactions is often very low, reflecting the fact that the two are following independent distributions.

Therefore, following Fader et al. (2005), the average expected transaction value for a customer with an average expenditure of mx across x transaction is modeled using a gamma distribution with scale parameter γ as follows:

$$E(M/p,q,\gamma,m_x,x) = \frac{(\gamma + m_x x)p}{px + q - 1}$$
$$= \left[\frac{(q-1)}{px+q-1}\right]\frac{\gamma p}{q-1} + \left[\frac{px}{px+q-1}\right]m_x$$

The model parameters (p, q) can be estimated using standard numerical optimization tools.

5.2.5 *Prediction*

The final predicted money value for each customer is calculated by combining the above three estimated values, that is,

$$\text{PRFM} = P(\text{active}) * E(\text{transaction}) * E(\text{money value})$$

where PRFM is the predicted money value for a customer over a specified future time period; *P*(active) is the recency factor, which is the estimated probability of being active in the specified future time period; *E*(transaction) is the frequency factor, i.e., expected number of transaction in the specified future time period; and *E* (money value) is the monetary factor, i.e., average money value for the specified future time period.

5.2.6 *Estimation*

There is no standard routine available in SAS to estimate the DGP-based models. One needs to write a program using maximum likelihood routine PROC NLMIXED available in SAS.

5.3 Data

To test the model, we applied it to three large retail consumer finance businesses from the USA, Europe, and Asia, respectively. Typically, the analysis considers two-year time window for the data, which is further split into observation and prediction window as given in Fig. 5.1.[2] The observation window data are used to develop the model, while the prediction (or target) window data are used to test the performance of the model. The accounts are flagged as "inactive" if they have zero

[2]However for European retail, we had only 7 months of performance data.

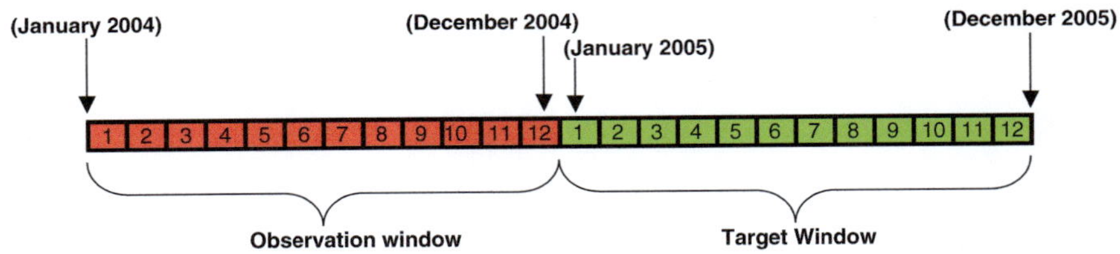

Fig. 5.1 Time window for data

purchases throughout the time period considered and only the active accounts are considered for developing the models. This active set of data is further split into development and validation at 70:30. The final sets of development samples have 51597, 149417, and 193858 observations, while the validation sample has 23327, 65096, and 84027 observations for the USA-, Europe-, and Asia-based retails, respectively.

5.3.1 Variables Used

As mentioned earlier, in contrast to many existing approaches, the model uses only three key customer attributes: recency, frequency, and monetary values. The recency is defined as the time that has elapsed since the customer made his most recent purchase. The frequency captures the total number of purchases that a customer has made within a designated period of time, while the monetary value denotes the average purchase amount of each customer.

5.4 Results and Retail Strategy Booster

5.4.1 Model Results and Validation

The results of the proposed model showing the lift for development and validation sample are provided in Fig. 5.2.

The top 3 deciles from the estimated PRFM model capture 56.1 % of total future purchase for the development sample for US data, 54.4 % for Europe, and 53.3 % for Asia data. Similarly, for the validation sample, it captures 56.4, 54.3, and 53.2 % for the US, Europe, and Asia data, respectively.

Further, the lift curves of the models for recency (R), frequency (F), and monetary (M) are shown in Fig. 5.3 to compare the overall model lift with that of the constituent models.

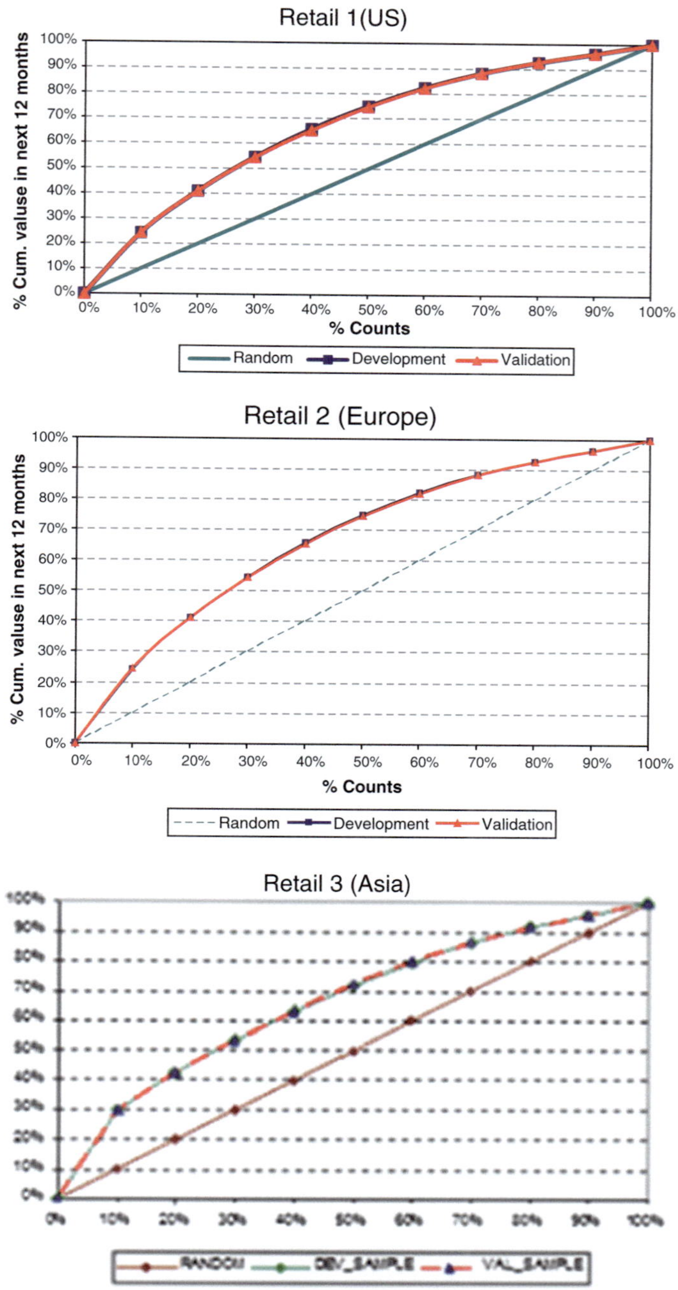

Fig. 5.2 Model lift of PRFM model

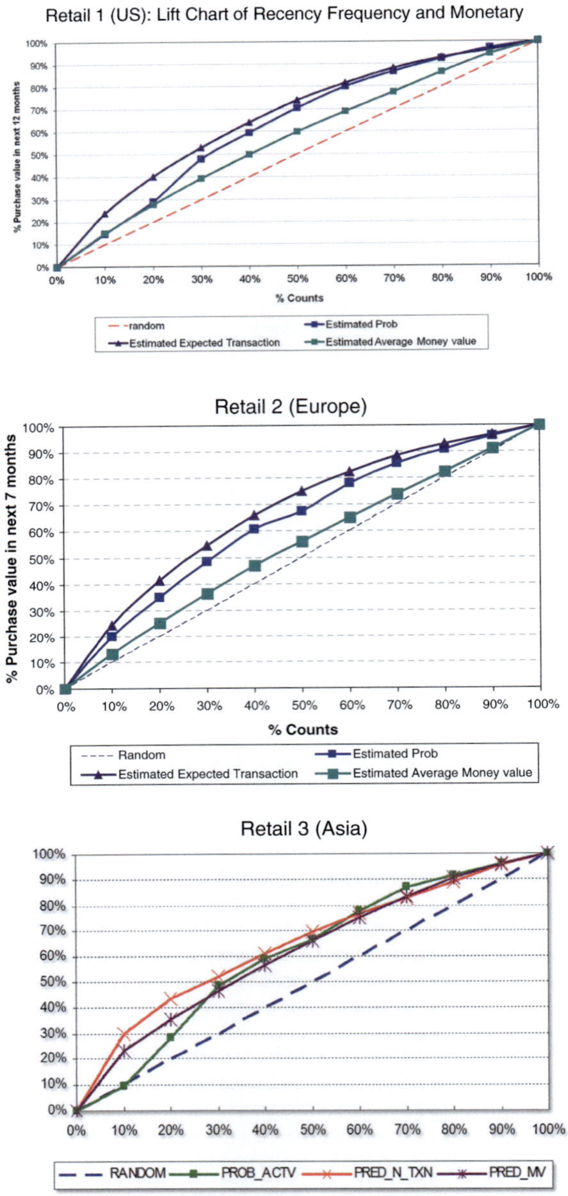

Fig. 5.3 Model lift for individual R, F, and M models

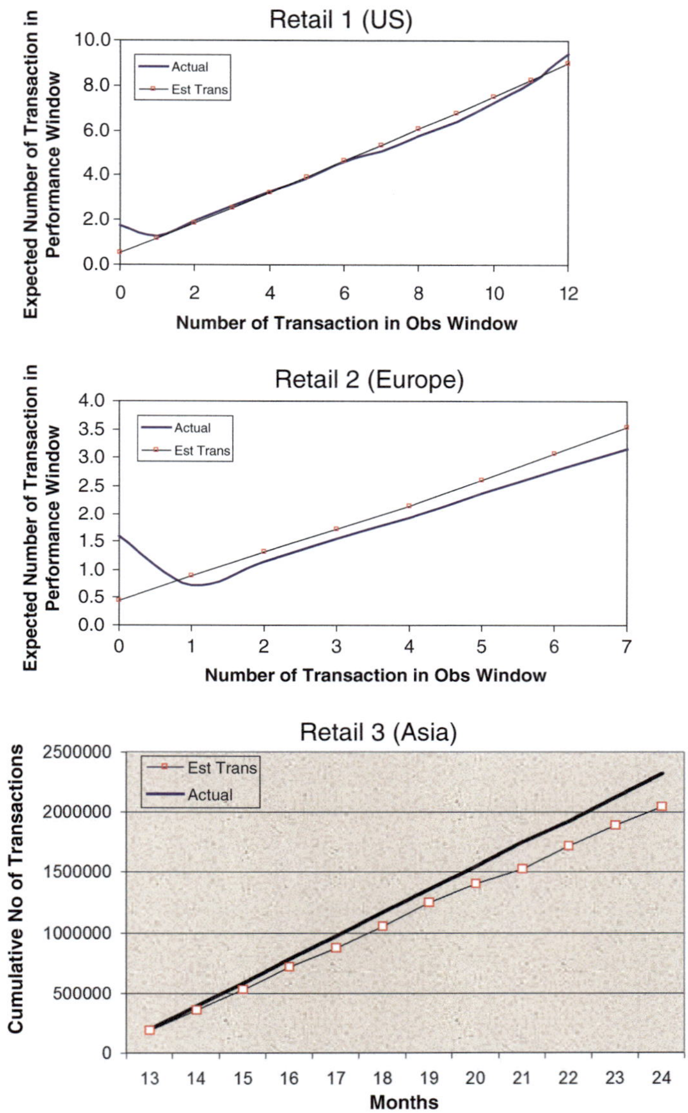

Fig. 5.4 Validation of conditional expectations of purchasing

For US data analysis, the probability of active model captures 47.8 % of the active customer in the top 3 deciles, expected number of transactions model captures 52.9 % of total transactions in the top 3 deciles, and the average money value model captures 39.3 % of the total purchase in the top 3 deciles individually, indicating that the combined effect of these three models serves to produce a more powerful predictive model. A similar lift is seen for other two markets as well.

For Europe, probability of active model captures 48 % in the top 3 deciles, expected number of transactions model captures 54.7 % in the top 3 deciles, and the average money value model captures 36.4 % in the top 3 deciles individually.

Similarly for Asia, probability of active model captures 48.7 % in the top 3 deciles, expected number of transactions model captures 52.2 % in the top 3 deciles, and the average money value model captures 46.4 % in the top 3 deciles individually.

Finally, three separate validation results are provided in the following figures to corroborate the performance of individual models, which are combined to get the final PRFM.

Figure 5.4 shows the predicted individual-level buying behavior in the future period (prediction window), suggesting a very strong predictive power for all three retails.

Further validation of actual versus estimated average transactions and percentage spend presented in Tables 5.1 and 5.2 reveals equally strong predictive power with very low error rate for all three cases. Additionally, an out-of-sample validation is carried out for the US-based retail. Figure 5.5 shows a close match of the expected cumulative numbers of transaction to the observed numbers indicating a very low forecast error.

Third and final validation is done through the concordance measure. Concordance is calculated as a percentage of number of exact sequence match between customers' observed and predicted transaction in the prediction window. A high concordance in all three cases (viz. 65 % for USA, 62 % for Europe, and 64 % for Asia data) not only reveals the power of the model to predict the events of purchase and total number of such events, but also the exact time sequence of the event of purchase in the performance window.

Table 5.1 Average number of transactions—actual versus estimated

Retail 1 (USA)			Retail 2 (Europe)			Retail 3 (Asia)		
Average number of transactions			Average number of transactions			Average number of transactions		
Decile	Estimated	Actual	Decile	Estimated	Actual	Decile	Estimated	Actual
1	6.4	6.2	1.0	5.5	5.0	1.0	8.7	9.2
2	5.7	5.6	2.0	4.5	4.1	2.0	8.8	9.1
3	5.3	5.2	3.0	3.9	3.5	3.0	8.9	9.3
4	4.8	4.7	4.0	3.3	3.0	4.0	8.9	9.3
5	4.3	4.3	5.0	2.9	2.6	5.0	8.8	9.1
6	3.7	3.7	6.0	2.4	2.2	6.0	8.6	8.9
7	2.9	3.0	7.0	2.0	1.8	7.0	8.2	8.4
8	2.1	2.1	8.0	1.6	1.4	8.0	7.5	7.6
9	1.1	1.3	9.0	1.2	1.1	9.0	6.1	6.0
10	0.7	1.7	10.0	0.8	1.1	10.0	2.4	2.3
Overall	3.7	3.7	Overall	2.8	2.5	Overall	7.7	7.9

Table 5.2 Average % spend—actual versus estimated

Retail 1 (USA)			Retail 2 (Europe)			Retail 3 (Asia)		
% of spend			% of spend			% of spend		
Decile	Estimated (%)	Actual (%)	Decile	Estimated (%)	Actual	Decile	Estimated (%)	Actual
1	30	28	1	18	26	1	34	32
2	20	18	2	19	19	2	17	15
3	16	15	3	16	15	3	13	13
4	14	13	4	13	13	4	11	12
5	12	11	5	12	11	5	10	11
6	10	9	6	10	10	6	9	10
7	8	8	7	8	8	7	8	9
8	6	6	8	7	6	8	7	7
9	3	5	9	5	6	9	6	6
10	2	6	10	3	6	10	5	6

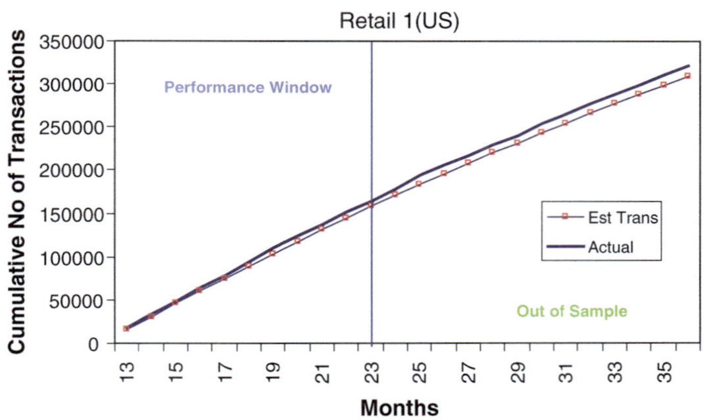

Fig. 5.5 Out-of-sample validation conditional expectations of purchasing

5.5 Conclusions

In contrast to many existing RFM-based models, we propose a set of model with strong underlying behavioral model, thereby providing a greater insight into the customer decisions.

This chapter following a DGP-based approach develops a predictive strategy based on past purchase transaction data. The approach basically predicts a customer's future purchase money value by combining the three key transaction factors, viz. recency, frequency, and monetary value which is further combined into a more powerful single predicted value (PRFM) for each customer. This represents an original contribution as many retailers and retail finance issuers are making decisions with RFM, but these are anchored on a static metric based on looking at past behavior and are not predictive in nature. Furthermore, when they do try to render RFM predictive, the methods are often ad hoc and, therefore, are usually difficult to implement in practice. In addition, this chapter also helps to categorize the customers into different groups, such as natural shopper, low-value or high-value dormant customer, which in turn benefits the business to have customized marketing strategies.

The final and most important characteristic of this model is the extensibility. Though the models depend only on three key customer attributes, R, F, and M, it can be easily extended to incorporate other customer attributes of interest by running the algorithm for each subsegment. Suggestions for future research include the adaptation of these techniques to all types of general purpose revolving credit cards which are being issued by most banks and consumer finance companies. Since consumers are using these cards to make purchases at a variety of retail establishments, the issuers of these cards face some of the same challenges as retailers transformed in this case from retail sales to card utilization.

References

Davenport TH, Harris JG (2007) Competing on analytics: the new science of winning. Harvard Business School Press

DeSarbo W, Ramaswamy V (1994) CRISP: customer response based iterative segmentation procedures for response modeling in direct marketing. J Direct Mark 8(Summer):7–20

Fader PS, Hardie BGS, Berger PD (2004) Customer-base analysis with discrete-time transaction data. Social Science Research Network (SSRN), Electronic publishing, Sept 2004

Fader PS, Hardie BGS, Lee KL (2005) RFM and CLV: using iso-value curves for customer base analysis. J Mark Res XLII

Schmittlein DC, Morrison DG, Colombo R (1987) Counting your customers: who are they and what will they do next? Manage Sci 33(1)

Schultz D (1995) The technological challenges to traditional direct marketing. J Direct Mark 9 (Winter):5–7

Chapter 6
Mitigating Sample Selection Bias Through Customer Relationship Management

Saumitra N. Bhaduri, V. Anuradha and David Fogarty

The customers you want to attract don't respond, and the ones you don't want to attract do.
Richard E. Mirman, Chief Marketing Officer
Harrah's Entertainment, Levey (2002, p. 1).

Abstract In direct marketing campaign, response models are often developed only based on the data of selected population. Since the propensity to respond depends on selection, this introduces a possibility of bias in the estimates of the response model. This chapter tries to apply a bivariate probit model with partial observability to correct the bias arising due to the sample selection and has applied the proposed model to a non-risk situation, viz. marketing campaign. This represents an original contribution as most marketing quantitative professionals to date have not been concerned with this sample selection bias due to the unstructured nature of applying models in a marketing context and also the fact that risk modeling approaches have had more time to mature from a research standpoint. Apart from addressing the selection bias, the model has helped to identify the customers who are likely to respond if selected for mailing which has led to a significant expansion of the existing mailing universe. This has a direct financial benefit to the home lending firm as it will serve to increase their customer share of wallet and subsequent profits.

6.1 Introduction

Successful customer relationship management (CRM) begins with the acquisition of right customers and organizes itself along the line of customer life cycle, including development (cross-sell/up-sell) and retention. All of these CRM efforts combined should lead to an increased "share of wallet" for the customer in a highly competitive environment. Historically, many researchers on CRM issues had focused on the identification, valuation, and retention of good customers (e.g., Dowling 2002; Rigby et al. 2002; Verhoef 2003; Winer 2001).

This chapter contains contributions from V. Anuradha, Madras School of Economics, Chennai, India.

S.N. Bhaduri and D. Fogarty, *Advanced Business Analytics*,
DOI 10.1007/978-981-10-0727-9_6

CRM managers generally put a significant amount of effort to find out who the best customers are and how to identify similar set of new customers who would be loyal and profitable. Therefore, a firm needs to invest sufficient amount of effort into the customer selection process and to develop strategies to avoid "adverse selection" and costly screening. In a direct marketing campaign scenario, the response models used for selection are often constructed using the data of selected population. Since the information of the non-selected population is generally ignored, it leads to a bias in the model parameters of the response model. This predicament is commonly known as sample selection bias and is closely linked with most of the marketing models developed for consumer finance loans or insurance. Hence, it is important to identify such bias, and this chapter proposes a methodology to correct the bias that might have caused due to the sample selection.

Further, any scoring model that is used to make (accept/reject) decisions will slowly deteriorate over time and will in due course have to be replaced (Hand 1998). Also, if the models are not updated regularly to capture the population shift and the possible changes in the underlying population characteristics, the predictive power of the original model will deteriorate. Besides this, if only data on accepted population are used to update the model, sample selection bias will give rise to question the validity of the new model. Hence, researchers have developed statistical methodologies to study the extent to which sample selection bias affects the performance of the model (e.g., Copas and Li 1997; Vella 1992), and they also continue to improve the selection techniques (e.g., Copas and Li 1997; Greene 1998; Feedler 1999). Some of the key contributions for handling selection problems are Heckman's (1979) two-stage bivariate probit model and Meng and Schmidt's (1985) bivariate probit model with partial observability to correct the selection bias.

Interestingly, a similar technique known as "reject inference" has been used to address the selection bias in risk analytics. This technique attempts to get additional data for the rejected applicants or tries to infer the missing information. Reject inference is a technique that is widely used by risk analysts in the development of risk default models known in the consumer finance industry as scorecards, although it has not been given extensive treatment in the literature. Henley (1997) describes two important reasons for needing reject inference as being the potential bias being introduced if a sample consisting only of accepted applicants is used to construct a new scorecard and also in order to obtain an accurate estimate of the portion of potential goods (from the full applicant population) being rejected by the existing scorecard. In addition, other unknown aspects of the structure of the reject population may provide further reasons for needing reject inference. Eisenbeis (1978) reported that using a model based solely on the truncated population of accepted applicants can frequently generate misleading results. Other authors, including Hsia (1978), Reichert et al. (1983), Joanes (1993, 1994), Hand (1998), have highlighted the possible bias that can result from using a sample of accepted applicants to build a scorecard with which to assess the full applicant population.

The process of reject inference has usually been used to reduce the bias by inferring the true status of the rejects often with mixed results due to the subjectivity of many of the current methods. Therefore, the technique presented in this chapter also provides a less subjective alternative to “reject inference” method.

Finally, although the primary focus of the chapter is to address the sample selection bias, the application of this chapter can be extended to develop a CRM solution to the twin problems of adverse selection and costly screening. In this chapter, we suggest a practical method for effectively implementing cross-selling activities to target its marketing efforts better that can help in improving the response rate (Dowling 2002).

A typical example of adverse selection in marketing campaign would involve selecting prospects who are less likely to respond, while rejecting prospects who are likely to respond for a given marketing campaign (Yong and Thomas 2005). Unfortunately, in firms’ attempts to attract new customers, they often draw responses from bad customers, who the firm wants to avoid leading to adverse selection. A classic example of such adverse selection is “price butterflies,” who chase deep discounts from one Web site to the other (Reichheld and Schefter 2000). The online grocer typically faces 75 % of its customers who are bargain hunters and benefit significantly by avoiding them. Moreover, the problem gets more compounded by requesting a response to an offer from an existing customer, and then rejecting him, the company loses its loyalty or good relationship with the customer as represented by customer equity built up over time. Therefore, it is critical for the CRM managers to solicit the best customers and find new customers who will be similarly loyal and profitable. To this end, the joint selection method presented in this chapter helps to achieve this objective.

In this chapter, we try to apply the Meng and Schmidt (1985) selection model to correct the bias for one of the leading Europe home lending businesses and hence improve the customer base and response rates. The remainder of this chapter is organized as follows. Section 6.2 reviews the methodology of bivariate probit models; Sect. 6.3 describes the data used for the analysis; Sect. 6.4 discusses the results; Sect. 6.5 throws light on strategies based on bivariate probit analysis; and Sect. 6.6 summarizes the chapter.

6.2 Methodology

Due to the large quantity of customers and large amounts of customer data available from the operational systems, many decisions in a consumer finance businesses are made through the use of statistically based scoring models. This chapter tries to address one of the basic problems in the consumer finance business involving declining performance of their scoring models over a period of time. This deterioration might happen because of sample selection bias, or if the existing model is not updated regularly to reflect the changes in the underlying population characteristics.

Generally, the sample selection bias arises due to a difference between the sampling distribution and population distribution. The differences are commonly observed in credit scoring, marketing response problems, where the performance is observed only on the accepted or selected population and not on the entire population.

The sample selection problem can be distributed into three types based on the bias they create: First, when the sample is representative of the whole population, the bias is least. Second, although the sample is drawn only from accepted applicants, it is assumed that the distribution pattern in the accepted region can be extended to that of rejected region through either observation or assumption leading to limited bias. Third, when the sample is drawn from the subpopulation of accepted applicants, it is assumed that the distribution of the accepted applicant population is different from that of the rejected applicant population indicating a possibility of critical bias.

Following Meng and Schmidt (1985), we approach the sample selection bias in a two-stage procedure. In a typical marketing campaign scenario, the first stage constitutes business decision whether to send a mail to a customer which can be captured by the selection equation. In the second stage, the response (accept/reject) status is observed which is captured by the response equation.

6.2.1 Simultaneous Approach to Correct the Selection Bias

Before describing the Meng and Schmidt's (1985) partial observability model, it may be useful to start with a generic bivariate probit model.

Let there be two binary-dependent variables $y^j, j = 1, 2$; each of this generated by a probit equation; and the errors are correlated. Thus, we have the model as follows:

$$y^{1*} = X\beta_1 + \varepsilon_1$$

$$y^{2*} = X\beta_2 + \varepsilon_2$$

where y^{j*} are unobservable and are related to the binary-dependent variables y^j by the rule

$$y^j = 1, \text{ if } y^{j*} > 0$$

$$y^j = 0, \text{if } y^{j*} \leq 0 \qquad \text{where } j = 1, 2$$

The error terms ε_1 and ε_2 are assumed to be standard bivariate normal with correlation ρ.

In the case of partial observability, the choices y_1 and y_2 are partially observed, specifically the case where both binary variables are taking the value as "1". Hence, instead of observing X_i, y_{i1}, and y_{i2}, it will be observed only as X_i and Z_i, where $Z_i = y_{i1} * y_{i2}$, $i = 1, 2, \ldots N$, that is,

$$z_i = 1, \text{ if } y_{i1} = 1 \text{ and } y_{i2} = 1$$

z_i = 0, otherwise.

The situation arises when we observe the final outcome of two decision processes which lead to a single conclusion. The log-likelihood function for Meng and Schmidt's model is given as follows:

$$\begin{aligned} \text{Log}\, L = & \textstyle\sum_{y1=1,y2=1} \ln \Phi_2\,[\beta_1\, x_{i1}, \beta_2\, x_{i2}, \rho] \\ & + \textstyle\sum_{y2=1,y1=0} \ln \Phi_2\,[-\beta_1\, x_{i1}, \beta_2\, x_{i2}\,, -\rho] \\ & + \textstyle\sum_{y2=0} \ln\,[-\Phi(\beta_2\, x_{i2}) \end{aligned} \quad \Bigg\}\ \text{both variables observed)}$$

Applying this to the marketing campaign example, we get

$$S = \beta_1 X_1 + \mu\,(\text{Selection Model})$$
$$R = \beta_2 X_2 + v\,(\text{Response Model})$$

Here, the dependent variable S is the observed selection for direct mailing, which can take the values of 0 or 1. The second dependent variable R is the observed response for selected customer with possible values of 0 or 1. μ and v are the error terms which follow a standard bivariate normal distribution with correlation ρ. Here, we need to note that the dependent variable R is observed only when the other dependent variable S has a value of 1, suggesting a partial observability with the selection bias. A statistically significant estimated value of ρ will indicate the presence of selection bias.

The parameters β_1, β_2, and ρ are estimated using the maximum likelihood method. Based on the MLE estimates, the probabilities P_{11}, P_{10}, P_{01}, and P_{00} are calculated, where P_{11} is the probability of response and selection, P_{10} is the probability of response and non-selection, P_{01} is the probability of selection and non-response, and P_{00} is the probability of non-selection and non-response. The probabilities P_{11}, P_{10}, P_{01}, and P_{00} are calculated as follows:

$$P_{i11} = \Phi_2(\beta_1'\, x_{i1},\ \beta_2'\, x_{i2}, \rho)$$

$$P_{i10} = \Phi(\beta_1'\, x_{i1}) - P_{i11}$$

$$P_{i01} = \Phi(\beta_2'\, x_{i2}) - P_{i11}$$

$$P_{i00} = P_{i11} - P_{i10} - P_{i01}$$

6.2.2 *Estimation*

Since no SAS Proc is available to run this model in the SAS Base version, a code has been written to estimate the model. However, an intermediate solution would be to use a specialized package (e.g., STATA) to do the estimation and implementation (score) using SAS.

6.3 Data

This chapter considers the data from one of the leading home lending business in Europe. The business has been facing a deterioration of its existing response model, which has resulted in a low response rate for their mailing campaigns. Historically, the business has been applying a selection model and has selected those customers falling under the top two deciles. Therefore, developing a new response model based only on the top two deciles of this selected data would suffer from a strong selectivity bias. The current direct mailing selection process is shown below.

Therefore to develop a new response model without selection bias, this chapter proposes a bivariate probit model with partial observability. The key objectives of the approach are as follows: first, to develop a new response model with better predictive power; second, to capture the customers who were not selected by the existing model but have the potential to respond and to lift the response rate as well as to expand the mailing volume.

The data set considered for analysis had a random sample of about 200,000 records, which was further divided into development and validation samples at the ratio of 60:40. The 120,000 data are used to develop the bivariate probit model, and it is validated on 80,000 observations.

6.3.1 Variables Used

This study uses all the observations to estimate the log likelihood. Initially, two models for selection and response, respectively, have been developed separately to get the initial parameters. Then, a joint bivariate probit model is run using these parameter estimates as the initial values. The selections of independent variables in the models are carried out after checking for correlation and multicollinearity. Finally, a robust check is performed on the proposed model by validating results with the validation sample.

6.4 Results

The initial estimates of selection model and response model are given in Tables 6.1 and 6.2. The estimate of joint bivariate probit model proposed in this chapter is given in Table 6.3. The corresponding lift curve is shown in Fig. 6.1. The sample size used in the estimation is 119,780. All the variables included in the model are

Table 6.1 Selection model—initial parameters

Variable	Description	Estimate	Wald-Chi square	*P* value
Intercept		−0.159579	33.8053	<0.0001
d3_Age_S	d3_Age_S = (48 < Age_S);	−0.278979	305.0025	<0.0001
d4_BAL	d4_BAL = (392.16 < BAL);	0.349721	203.293	<0.0001
d2_BAL_HIGHEST	d2_BAL_HIGHEST = (70.56 < BAL_HIGHEST ≤ 255);	−0.204479	148.4644	<0.0001
d3_clcode_s	d3_clcode_s = (6 < clcode_s);	−0.321179	116.0282	<0.0001
d4_CREDIT_LIMIT	d4_CREDIT_LIMIT = (2000 < CREDIT_LIMIT);	0.495021	610.6209	<0.0001
d1_CREDIT_LIMIT	d1_CREDIT_LIMIT = (CREDIT_LIMIT ≤ 350);	−0.264079	149.8579	<0.0001
d5_EPCF11s	d5_EPCF11s = (31 < % of houses with one adult ≤ 39);	0.081121	15.9512	<0.0001
D5_FSC108s	D5_FSC108s = fixed term accounts unsecured loans worst status last 1 month IN (40, 44, 46, 47, 50, 60);	0.439621	767.8805	<0.0001
d2_JSC560s	D2_JSC560S = JSC560S IN (12, 14, 16, 18, 22, 24, 26, 28);	1.279421	1936.525	<0.0001
d3_JSC560s	D3_JSC560S = JSC560S IN (30, 32);	0.725321	1960.56	<0.0001
d2_LPCF18s	d2_LPCF18s = (0 < percentage of houses with cards ≤ 42);	0.390121	288.8908	<0.0001
d3_LSC303s	d3_LSC303s = (3 < number of accounts opened last 24 months ≤ 4);	0.440421	347.9238	<0.0001
d4_LSC303s	d4_LSC303s = (4 < number of accounts opened last 24 months);	0.811221	1989.213	<0.0001
d3_LSC546s	d3_LSC546s = (7 < number of months on 0 number of arrears in last 12 months ≤ 9);	0.388121	228.9905	<0.0001
d3_LSC547s	d3_LSC547s = (18 < number of months on 0 number of arrears in last 24 months ≤ 22);	0.201021	122.1609	<0.0001
d2_LSC585s	d2_LSC585s = (2 < number of companies used ≤ 5);	−0.157779	70.1979	<0.0001
d2_prod_s	d2_prod_s = (0 < prod_s ≤ 1);	−1.818279	6004.849	<0.0001
d4_TIME_CUR_ADDRESS_APP	d4_TIME_CUR_ADDRESS_APP = (506 < TIME_CUR_ADDRESS_APP ≤ 1600);	−0.302579	280.1538	<0.0001
d5_TIME_CUR_ADDRESS_APP	d5_TIME_CUR_ADDRESS_APP = (1600 < TIME_CUR_ADDRESS_APP);	−0.421679	329.3846	<0.0001

Note Any further description of the independent variables cannot be provided due to the confidentiality agreement with data provider

Table 6.2 Response model—initial parameters

Variable	Description	Estimate	Wald-Chi square	*P* value
Intercept		−3.4190	1516.8025	<0.0001
d1_BAL_HIGHEST	d1_BAL_HIGHEST = (BAL_HIGHEST ≤ 121);	−0.4400	19.4174	<0.0001
d2_clcode_s	d2_clcode_s = (1 < clcode_s ≤ 3);	−0.2493	15.1531	<0.0001
D5_FSC308s	D5_FSC308s = fixed term accounts mortgages and secured loans worst status last 1 month IN (40, 44, 46, 47, 50, 60);	0.7212	104.403	<0.0001
D5_FSC402s	D5_FSC402s = fixed term accounts mortgages and secured loans worst status last 3 months before settled IN (40, 44, 46, 47, 50, 60);	0.2671	14.6618	0.0001
d5_indebtedness_score	d5_indebtedness_score = (419 < indebtedness_score);	−1.5447	62.6805	<0.0001
d4_indebtedness_score	d4_indebtedness_score = (320 < indebtedness_score ≤ 419);	−0.7288	71.0056	<0.0001
d4_LSC303s	d4_LSC303s = (6 < number of accounts opened last 24 months);	0.3522	24.0786	<0.0001
d4_LSC617s	d4_LSC617s = (9 < worst status code ≤ 20);	−0.3498	19.7435	<0.0001
d5_LSC617s	d5_LSC617s = (20 < worst status code);	−0.7655	28.8911	<0.0001
d3_NAC137s	d3_NAC137s = (22 < aggregated revolving accounts utilization (%) last 6 months);	0.4245	38.2057	<0.0001
d5_NSC135s	d5_NSC135s = (64 < aggregated revolving accounts utilization (%) last 1 month);	0.6495	85.3557	<0.0001
d3_NSC135s	d3_NSC135s = (9 < aggregated revolving accounts utilization (%) last 1 month ≤ 28);	−0.4543	23.0788	<0.0001
d2_RISK_SCORE	d2_RISK_SCORE = (RISK_SCORE ≤ 285);	0.5360	53.5318	<0.0001
d5_RISK_SCORE	d5_RISK_SCORE = (456 < RISK_SCORE);	−0.5430	27.4703	<0.0001
d5_rn_evo3_score	d5_rn_evo3_score = (512 < rn_evo3_score);	−0.5857	16.9536	<0.0001
d4_TRAN_301_sum	d4_TRAN_301_sum = (680.09 < TRAN_301_sum);	0.3994	32.0845	<0.0001

Note Any further description of the independent variables cannot be provided due to the confidentiality agreement with data provider

Table 6.3 Results of bivariate probit model

Variable	Description	Estimate	*t* value	Pr > |*t*|
Response model parameters				
Constant1		−1.6556	−28.22	<0.0001
d1_BAL_HIGHEST	d1_BAL_HIGHEST = (BAL_HIGHEST ≤ 121);	0.1282	3.81	0.0001
d2_clcode_s	d2_clcode_s = (1 < clcode_s ≤ 3);	−0.1004	−3.41	0.0006
D5_FSC308s	D5_FSC308s = fixed term accounts unsecured loans worst status last 1 month IN (40, 44, 46, 47, 50, 60);	−0.1553	−4.37	<0.0001
D5_FSC402s	D5_FSC402s = fixed term accounts mortgages and secured loans worst status last 3 months before settled IN (40, 44, 46, 47, 50, 60);	−0.2010	−4.61	<0.0001
d5_indebtedness_score	d5_indebtedness_score = (419 < indebtedness_score);	0.1694	5.04	<0.0001
d4_indebtedness_score	d4_indebtedness_score = (320 < indebtedness_score ≤ 419)	0.3382	10.09	<0.0001
d4_LSC303s	d4_LSC303s = (6 < number of accounts opened last 24 months);	−0.6319	−8.97	<0.0001
d4_LSC617s	d4_LSC303s = (4 < number of accounts opened last 24 months);	−0.2248	−5.07	<0.0001
d5_LSC617s	d5_LSC617s = (20 < worst status code);	0.2178	6.47	<0.0001
d3_NAC137s	d3_NAC137s = (22 < aggregated revolving accounts utilization (%) last 6 months);	−0.2523	−4.43	<0.0001
d5_NSC135s	d5_NSC135s = (64 < aggregated revolving accounts utilization (%) last 1 month);	0.3043	9.4	<0.0001
d3_NSC135s	d3_NSC135s = (9 < aggregated revolving accounts utilization (%) last 1 month ≤ 28)	−0.3513	−9.59	<0.0001
d2_RISK_SCORE	d2_RISK_SCORE = (RISK_SCORE ≤ 285)	0.1444	4.01	<0.0001
d5_RISK_SCORE	d5_RISK_SCORE = (456 < RISK_SCORE)	−0.2055	−5.06	<0.0001
d5_rn_evo3_score	d5_rn_evo3_score = (512 < rn_evo3_score)	−0.3083	−5.07	<0.0001
d4_TRAN_301_sum	d4_TRAN_301_sum = (680.09 < TRAN_301_sum)	0.1900	5.47	<0.0001
Rho	Correlation	−0.1563	−4.53	<0.0001
Selection model parameters				
Constant2		−0.1112	−6.98	<0.0001
d3_Age_S	d3_Age_S = (48 < Age_S);	0.0478	3.91	<0.0001
d4_BAL	d4_BAL = (392.16 < BAL);	0.2265	16.82	<0.0001

(continued)

Table 6.3 (continued)

Variable	Description	Estimate	*t* value	Pr > |*t*|
d2_BAL_HIGHEST	d2_BAL_HIGHEST = (70.56 < BAL_HIGHEST ≤ 255);	0.2324	15.32	<0.0001
d3_clcode_s	d3_clcode_s = (6 < clcode_s);	0.1255	11.7	<0.0001
d4_CREDIT_LIMIT	d4_CREDIT_LIMIT = (2000 < CREDIT_LIMIT);	−0.1733	−16.94	<0.0001
d1_CREDIT_LIMIT	d1_CREDIT_LIMIT = (CREDIT_LIMIT ≤ 350);	−0.1819	−11.07	<0.0001
d5_EPCF11s	d5_EPCF11s = (31 < percentage of houses with 1 adult ≤ 39);	0.2572	18.62	<.0001
D5_FSC108s	D5_FSC108s = fixed term accounts unsecured loans worst status last 1 month IN (40, 44, 46, 47, 50, 60);	0.7505	43.8	<.0001
d2_JSC560s	D2_JSC560S = JSC560S IN (12, 14, 16, 18, 22, 24, 26, 28);	−0.1624	−17.9	<0.0001
d3_JSC560s	D3_JSC560S = JSC560S IN (30, 32);	−0.2397	−18.48	<0.0001
d2_LPCF18s	d2_LPCF18s = (0 < percentage of houses with cards ≤ 42);	0.4248	44.85	<0.0001
d3_LSC303s	d3_LSC303s = (3 < number of accounts opened last 24 months ≤ 4);	−1.0711	−78.56	<0.0001
d4_LSC303s	d4_lsc303s = (4 < number of accounts opened last 24 months);	0.2626	28.3	<0.0001
d3_LSC546s	d3_LSC546s = (7 < number of months on 0 number of arrears in last 12 months ≤ 9);	0.2224	15.46	<0.0001
d3_LSC547s	d3_LSC547s = (18 < number of months on 0 number of arrears in last 24 months ≤ 22);	−0.0900	−8.65	<0.0001
d2_LSC585s	d2_LSC585s = (2 < number of companies used ≤ 5);	0.2900	24.49	<0.0001
d2_prod_s	d2_prod_s = (0 < prod_s ≤ 1);	0.4793	45.05	<0.0001
d4_TIME_CUR_ADDRESS_APP	d4_TIME_CUR_ADDRESS_APP = (506 < TIME_CUR_ADDRESS_APP ≤ 1600);	−0.1353	−11.24	<0.0001
d5_TIME_CUR_ADDRESS_APP	d5_TIME_CUR_ADDRESS_APP = (1600 < TIME_CUR_ADDRESS_APP);	−0.1114	−11.87	<0.0001

Note Any further description of the independent variables cannot be provided due to the confidentiality agreement with data provider

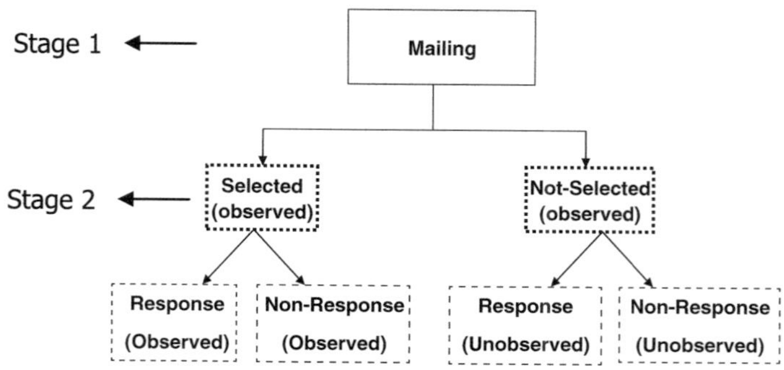

Fig. 6.1 Two-stage procedure

significant at 99.99 % level. Selection of variables is done through a routine multicollinearity check, having all VIFs less than 1.75. Some of the key explanatory variables are highest balance, credit limit, age, and risk score.

This model captures 82 % of responses in the top 2 deciles. Finally, the other probabilities, P10, P01, and P00, are calculated based on the formula provided earlier.

6.5 Understanding and Identifying the Likely Responders from Non-selected Base

Apart from developing a new response model, one of the primary objectives of the study is to understand the characteristics of the non-selected customers captured by P10. The distribution of P10 would help us to identify those who would have responded had they been selected. After rank ordering the accounts based on P10, a profiling is done for the customers falling under the top 2 deciles.

Some of the key characteristics of the customers falling in the top deciles are as follows. About 65 % of the accounts are in the age group between 28 and 48 years;

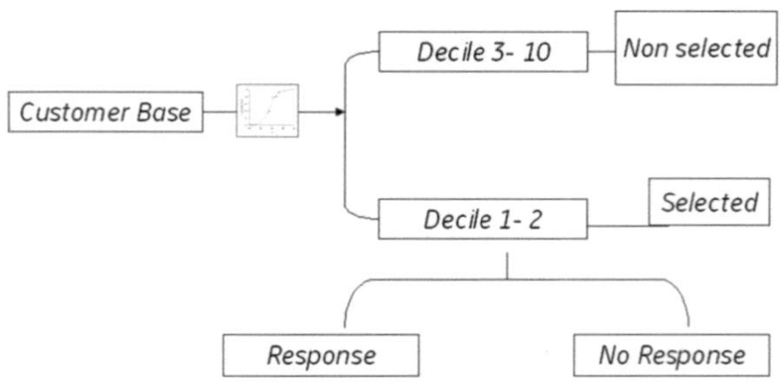

Fig. 6.2 Current direct mail selection process

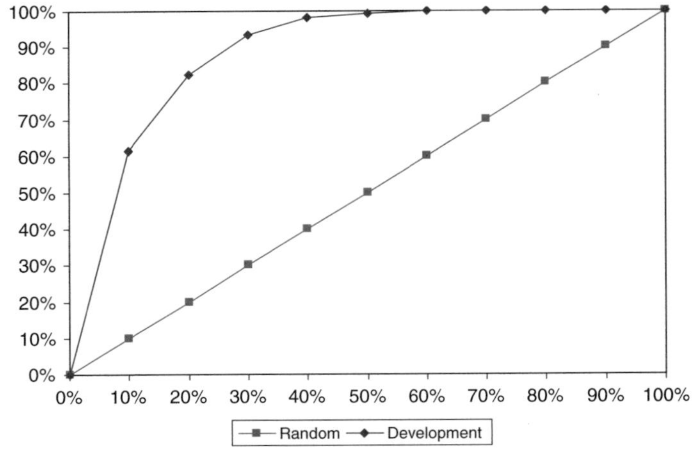

Fig. 6.3 Lift chart

43 % of accounts have greater than 4 accounts opened last 24 months; 39 % of accounts have less than 9 months on 0 number of arrears in last 12 months; number of different lenders the customer has for his accounts is greater than 11 for 41 % accounts; the age in months of most recently opened account is less than 5 for 46 % of accounts; aggregated revolving accounts utilization (%) last 1 month is greater than 64 % for 33 % of accounts; 61 % of accounts have at least one fixed term account on mortgage and secured loans (Figs. 6.2 and 6.3).

6.6 Conclusions

This chapter develops a bivariate probit with partial observability model to correct the sample selection bias and has applied the proposed model to a non-risk situation, viz. marketing campaign. This represents an original contribution as most marketing quantitative professionals to date have not been concerned with this sample selection bias. This is most likely due to the unstructured nature of applying models in a marketing context and also the fact that risk modeling approaches have been around longer, and therefore, most of the outstanding issues and challenges with them have had more time to mature from a research standpoint. Apart from addressing the selection bias, the model has helped to identify the customers who are likely to respond if selected for mailing which has led to a significant expansion of the existing mailing universe. This has a direct financial benefit to the home lending firm as it will serve to increase their customer share of wallet and subsequent profits. However, further research is necessary in order to test the power of this model with all proposed extensions for both non-risk and risk applications.

References

Copas JB, Li HG (1997) Inference for non-random samples (with discussion). J R Stat Soc, B 59:55–95

Dowling G (2002) Customer relationship management. In B2C markets, often less is more. Calif Manag Rev 44(3):87–104

Eisenbeis RA (1978) Pitfalls in the application of discriminant analysis in business, finance and economics. J Finan 32(3):875–900

Feelders AJ (1999) Credit scoring and reject inference with mixture models. Int J Intell Syst Account Finan Manag 8:271–279

Greene W (1998) Sample selection in credit-scoring models. Japan World Econ 10:299–316

Hand DJ (1998) Reject inference in credit operations. In: Mays E (ed) Credit risk modeling: design and application, pp 181–190. AMACOM

Heckman JJ (1979) Sample selection bias as a specification error. Econometrica 47:153–161

Henley WE (1997) The statistical aspects of credit scoring. Unpublished PhD. Dissertation, The Open University

Hsia DC (1978) Credit scoring and the equal credit opportunity act. Hastings Law J 30:371–448

Joanes DN (1993/1994) Reject inference applied to logistic regression for credit scoring. IMA J Math Appl Bus Ind 5(1):35–43

Meng C-L, Peter S (1985) On the cost of partial observation in the bivariate probit model. Int Econ Rev 26(1):71–85

Reichert AK, Cho CC, Wagner GM (1983) An examination of the conceptual issues involved in developing credit scoring models. J Bus Econ Stat 1:101–114

Reichheld FF (1996) The loyalty effect. Harvard Business School Press, Cambridge, MA

Reichheld FF, Phil S (2000) E-loyalty: your secret weapon on the web. Harvard Bus Rev 78:105–113

Rigby DK, Reichheld FF, Schefter P (2002) Avoid the four perils of CRM. Harvard Bus Rev 80 (February):5–11

Vella F (1992) Simple tests for sample selection bias in censored and discrete choice models. J Appl Econ 7:413–421

Verhoef PC (2003) Understanding the effect of customer relationship management efforts on customer retention and customer share development. J Market 67(October):30–45

Winer Russell S (2001) A framework for customer relationship management. Calif Manag Rev 43 (Summer):89–105

Young C, Thomas SG (2005) Reducing adverse selection through customer relationship management

Chapter 7
Enabling Incremental Gains Through Customized Price Optimization

Saumitra N. Bhaduri, V. Anuradha, Avanti George and David Fogarty

Abstract Price optimization solutions presented in this chapter provide an analytic approach that helps the business to improve margins and increase volumes. The chapter proposes a comprehensive pricing framework which not only maximizes short-term gains but also addresses critical value enhancing CRM issues, such as cross-sell, up-sell, and better life cycle management through retention. The significant contribution of the chapter involves developing a framework that explicitly and transparently takes into account the price response and adverse elasticity concepts. Also in order to successfully capture the consumer behavior, this chapter introduces advanced modeling techniques such as the double hurdle model, in contrast to the more traditional logistic models, and demonstrates its efficiency to model attrition and risk. Additionally, this chapter introduces a sophisticated clustering technique called "genetic algorithm" for segmentation analysis. Finally, based on the insights from this analysis, a dynamic optimization tool is developed to effectively improve the risk-adjusted profit for the business.

7.1 Introduction

Pricing has always been a key differentiator in all competitive markets, but it has gained further importance in the present environment with increased globalization and competition. Pricing has no longer remained a simple strategy of cutting prices or volume discounts; it has emerged as a strategy of applying the right prices to the right products at the right time to improve sales and to boost margin.

Ironically, many companies, even today, rely on outdated practices such as cost-plus or meet-the-competition to set their prices. Hence, the objective of this chapter is to develop a better approach, known as price optimization which can provide a quantitative means of setting prices that significantly improves margins and boosts profits.

This chapter contains contributions from V. Anuradha and Avanti George, Madras School of Economics, Chennai, India.

S.N. Bhaduri and D. Fogarty, *Advanced Business Analytics*,
DOI 10.1007/978-981-10-0727-9_7

The principle of price optimization involves maximization of profit by offering a price that matches the customer's willingness to pay while keeping the risk of attracting bad credit customers at bay. A research carried out by McKinsey found that a 1 % change in price could have an impact as great as 11 % on a company's operating profits.[1] Further, studies show that between 1 and 5 % of the value is lost across all industries because companies do not know enough about their customers' willingness to pay or do not have the ability to profit from this knowledge.

Analytical approaches for setting prices have been used successfully in various industries. The first comprehensive work on the concept, theories, and application of pricing and revenue optimization was introduced by Phillips (2005) in his book "Pricing and Revenue Optimization." Price optimization, a term often used interchangeably with profit-based pricing, is a method of finding the right price for a particular customer by channel, segment, geography, market, or product. However, most of the current applications relating to pricing optimization are in industries that operate more in a B2C environment such as airlines, retail, hotel, hospitality, insurance, and telecommunications. Price optimization was first developed in the USA more than three decades ago, specifically for the airline industry. These price optimization models were successfully applied to optimize fare mix, overbooking, upgrading, and balancing capacities. Similar benefits are realized in retail, insurance, and other industries.

While other industries have been utilizing price optimization since the 1970s, the financial services industry has only turned to price optimization in the last couple of years. The price optimization in the consumer finance business requires the ability to dynamically set prices based on the risk and the customer's propensity to use the product. Although various price optimization capabilities are currently available, they have several limitations: To begin with, many of the existing pricing solutions do not address both profit and volume objectives; moreover, they often ignore the possibility of tapping into new business flow and fail to counter the potential loss to competitors through reduced life cycle. Therefore, the objective of this chapter is to propose a comprehensive pricing framework which not only maximizes short-term gain but addresses critical value enhancing CRM issues such as cross-sell, up-sell, and better life cycle management through retention.

The objective of this chapter is threefold. Firstly, it introduces a comprehensive framework for price optimization for the consumer finance business, which addresses some of the important concerns such as adverse selection, early termination, cross-selling, and up-selling. Further, one of the salient contributions of this chapter is to understand the customer response elasticities (i.e., the extent to which demand falls as price increases) and adverse selection elasticities (i.e., the extent to which credit quality falls as price increases). In contrast to many existing pricing optimization solutions, the proposed framework explicitly and transparently takes into account these elasticity concepts. And the proposed optimum solution is generated by considering the variations in elasticity across segments and optimally

[1] www.zilliant.com/downloads/CMO_1104.pdf.

balancing the customer preferences with the risks involved. Secondly, it introduces "state-of-the-art" modeling techniques to effectively capture the consumer behavior. Specifically, in contrast to the more traditional logistic models, this chapter introduces sophisticated models such as the double hurdle models and demonstrates its efficiency to model attrition and risk.

This chapter primarily focuses on price optimization for the financial industry. This chapter is structured as follows. Section 7.2 describes the methodology adopted in this chapter; Sect. 7.3 provides the generic price optimization framework, along with the results of a simulation study; Sect. 7.4 depicts the dynamic price optimization tool; and Sect. 7.5 concludes with a summary.

7.2 Methodology

7.2.1 Customized Price Optimization Solution

In general, the goal of the business is to maximize the "total net revenue" which is the sum of all the margins of all products sold during a specified time period. Typically, the margin is defined as the difference between the price of the product and the cost. Abstracting to a single line of product, the total net revenue can be represented as follows:

$$m(r) = (r - c)\,L - l\,(r)\,L \tag{7.1}$$

where, left-hand side, $m(r)$ is the total net revenue, "r" is the price per unit (i.e., APR[2]), "c" is the cost per unit, $l\,(r)$ is the probability of default, and "L" is the number of units (i.e., the loan volume).

Note, the margin $(r - c)$ is a strictly increasing function, while the $l(r)$ is assumed to be a concave function, signifying the adverse selection problem that arises as a result of attracting low credit quality customers at a high price. Therefore, the total net revenue is an upward sloping, inverted U-shaped function of price as shown in Fig. 7.1. The peak of the curve is the maximum total net revenue the business can attain in the present time period, and p* is the optimal price that would maximize the total net revenue.

7.2.2 The Generic Construct

Specifically, the customized pricing problem for a particular offer therefore can be set up as follows:

[2]APR is the annualized percentage rate.

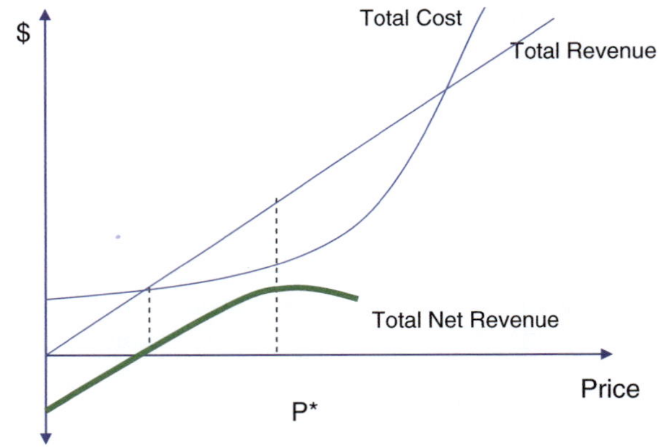

Fig. 7.1 Total net revenue function

Fig. 7.2 Expected total net revenue

$$\text{Max}\, \tau(r) = [\lambda(r)][m(r)] + [1 - \lambda(r)][m(r)] \tag{7.2}$$

where $\tau(r)$ is the expected total net revenue at price "r," $[\lambda(r)]$ is the response function (i.e., probability of response at price "r"), and $[m(r)]$ is the total net revenue at price "r." Since the response function $[\lambda(r)]$ is a continuous, downward sloping function of price, the expected total net revenue $[\tau(r)]$ will be an inverted U-shape with an optimal price r^* which maximizes the total net revenue. Figure 7.2 is the depiction of the expected total net revenue function.

The unconstrained optimization problem setup in Eq. 7.2 can be solved by taking the derivative of τ and setting it equal to zero.

$$\tau'(r) = [\lambda'(r)Lr] + [\lambda(r)L] - [\lambda'(r)Lc] - [\lambda'(r)l(r)L] - [\lambda(r)l'(r)L]$$

$$\tau'(r) = 0$$

This results in the following:

$$e_r = -\frac{\lambda'(r^*)\cdot r^*}{\lambda(r^*)} = \frac{r^* - e_{as}\cdot l(r^*)}{r^* - c - l(r^*)} \tag{7.3}$$

where e_{as} is the adverse selection elasticity, defined as a percentage change in the loss due to a 1 % change in the price, and e_r is the response price elasticity. Therefore, the optimality is achieved when the customer's response elasticity e_r is equal to inverse of the total net revenue margin ratio where the response elasticity is defined as the percentage change in the probability of response due to 1 % change in price. In other words,

$$\text{Response elasticity at optimal price} = 1/(\text{net total revenue margin ratio})$$

7.2.3 Price Differentiation

The price differentiation as an ability to charge differentiated price is often used as a method of augmenting business profit. The price differentiation in consumer finance business would typically involve charging different prices to different segments of customers based on their willingness to pay. Therefore, one of the objectives of the proposed price optimization solution is to divide the market into various segments, such that a higher price can be charged to the high willingness to pay segments and lower price to the low willingness to pay segments. However, the ability to effectively segment the market will require "state-of-the-art" analytics to identify opportunities to charge differentiated price on the basis of willingness to pay, risk, and profitability of various segments. For a two segment scenario, the optimization problem can be defined as follows:

$$\begin{aligned} m^*(v) = \max_{r_i r_j} & [(r_i - c)\,L\,(r_i; s_1) - l(r_i; s_1)L\,(r_i; s_1)] + [(r_j - c)\,L(r_j; s_2) \\ & - l(r_j; s_2)L(r_j; s_2)] \end{aligned}$$

where s_1 and s_2 are two segments that belong to market "S".

7.3 Price Optimization Framework

Setting the right price for a consumer finance business is a complex decision. There are many parameters that come into play in determining the right prices for the right customer, such as term of the product (e.g., loan and mortgage), the size of the deal (e.g., amount borrowed), the propensity to early repayment, propensity to default, and the adverse selection.

Unfortunately, very few existing pricing solutions or companies approach the pricing in a systematic manner, resulting in a poorly managed process involving contradictory decisions based more often on intuition than on data. A senior executive of one of the leading US automakers is cited by the Boston Consulting

Group as saying, "we have over six thousand financial controllers watching our costs, but less than one hundred people working on price management."

Consequently, one of the important objectives of this chapter is to present a comprehensive pricing framework for consumer finance business by introducing many relevant drivers of risk-adjusted profit such as adverse selection elasticities, response elasticities, propensity of early payment, effective segmentation, other CRM opportunities such as cross-sell (e.g., insurance, additional cards) and up-sell (e.g., refinance and line of credit), regulatory constraints, and the competition. The following section briefly introduces each of these concepts and the analytical techniques proposed by this chapter to capture the consumer behavior.

7.3.1 *Adverse Selection*

Unfortunately, in an attempt to attract new customers, the businesses often obtain responses from the type of customers which they wish to avoid (Yong and Gruca 2005). This is generally referred as the adverse selection problem. The chapter proposes a logit function to capture the propensity of default $l(r)$ as follows:

$$l(r) = \frac{1}{1 + e^{(\alpha + \beta r)}}$$

where α and β are the parameters of the model and r is the price. The slope $l'(r)$ and the adverse selection elasticity e_{as} for the logit bid-response function are defined as follows:

$$l'(r) = \frac{-\beta e^{(\alpha + \beta r)}}{(1 + e^{(\alpha + \beta r)})^2} = -\beta l(r)(1 - l(r))$$

$$e_{as}(r) = l'(r)\, r / l(r) = -\beta r(1 - l(r))$$

7.3.2 *The Response Model*

A response model predicts the likelihood that a targeted customer would respond to the price offered. The main objective, of many existing risk-based pricing approaches, is to identify the high-risk customers and charge them higher rates. However, they often fail to take into account one of the key elements underlying an effective optimal pricing with maximum return, which is the customer price elasticities. Since most of the consumer finance business has abundant data on

Fig. 7.3 Bid-response curve

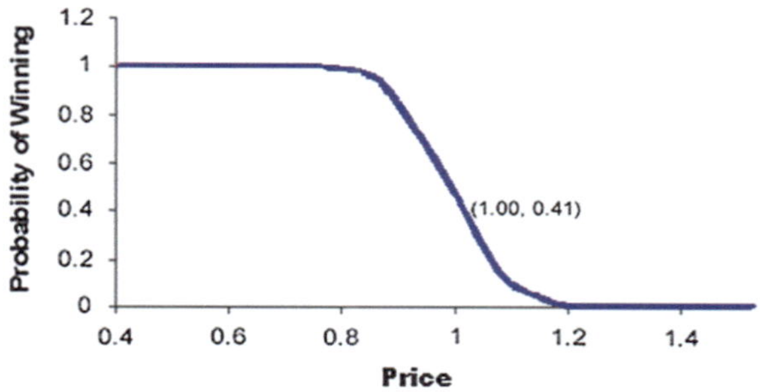

"customer rejects",[3] it provide a unique opportunity to apply state-of-the-art techniques to predict the individual's propensity to respond to a particular price and corresponding elasticities.

Several chapters, such as Freidman (1956), Gates (1967), Lawrence (2003), develop bid-response models, where price is the only attribute for winning a bid and the single objective is that of maximizing profits. Morin and Clough (1969) further build on these models, giving recent data more importance, thereby identifying key competitors and capturing sensitivity to changes in strategy. Lilien et al. (1992) provide a sketch of competitive pricing where the firm makes a trade-off between the probability of winning a bid and the margin earned. King and Mercer (1991) discuss estimation techniques for determining these bid-to-cost ratios. In addition, Papaioannou and Cassaigne (2000) develop the price response function, which accommodates multiple objectives by incorporating both price and non-price attributes. Phillips (2005) develops bid-response models using logit functions; while Agrawal and Ferguson (2006) extend this further to include the competitor's price which incorporates the competitive dynamics.

This chapter introduces a customized pricing response model which provides a probability of winning for every possible offer, allowing the business to balance a decreasing margin with an increasing win probability needed to optimize the price (Phillips 2005).

This chapter proposes an S-shaped response function which can represented using different functional forms, such as logit, probit, or power functions. However, finally, we select the logit function as it provides the most flexibility form and is defined as follows:

$$\lambda(r) = \frac{1}{1 + e^{(\alpha + \beta r)}}$$

where α and β are the parameters of the model and r is the price. An example of the bid-response function curve is shown in Fig. 7.3. The slope $\lambda'(r)$ and price elasticity e_r for the logit response function are represented as follows:

---

[3]Data on those candidates who have applied, but then, decided not to accept an offer.

$$\lambda'(r) = \frac{-\beta e^{(\alpha+\beta r)}}{(1+e^{(\alpha+\beta r)})^2} = -\beta\lambda(r)(1-\lambda(r))$$

$$e_r = \lambda'(r)\, r/\lambda(r) = -\beta r(1-\lambda(r))$$

This price response function is estimated using a typical maximum likelihood estimate of a general logit model, with $Y_i = 1$, if the customer accepts the offer, else $Y_i = 0$. Hence, the log-likelihood function is represented as follows:

$$\max_{\alpha,\beta} \ln(L(\alpha,\beta)) = \sum_{i=1,n} \ln\left[\frac{Y_i}{1+e^{(\alpha+\beta r_i)}} + \frac{(1-Y_i)\, e^{(\alpha+\beta r_i)}}{1+e^{(\alpha+\beta r_i)}}\right]$$

By applying the maximum likelihood estimation approach, the parameter values of α and β can be estimated.

7.3.3 Early Settlement

Given the current competitive market conditions, early termination or attrition is one of the major problems in consumer finance industry. Recent research has shown that the customer retention has a significant impact on firm's profitability: Gupta et al. (2004) find that 1 % improvement in retention may lead to an increase in firm value by 5 %. Therefore, any effective pricing framework should adequately address the early termination problem. One of the salient features of this chapter is to develop methods and techniques to precisely identify the potential attrition in a cost-effective manner.

Attrition models are simply a statistical prediction of which customers are likely to remain loyal and which are likely to leave. Historically, logistic regression technique has been used for attrition model, but this has some significant disadvantages. A major limitation of this technique is that it ignores the simple observation that customers attrite at different points in times in their life cycle and hence undermines the dynamic element in customer attrition behavior, which is one of key elements. Therefore, this chapter proposes a new class of models known as double hurdle models (originally proposed by Cragg (1971)), which allows for modeling the potential attrition and the extent of attrition separately.

Advanced Attrition Model—Double Hurdle Approach

As the name suggests, a consumer in a double hurdle framework must cross two hurdles in order to attrite. The "first hurdle" needs to be crossed in order to be a potential attritor. Given that the borrower is a potential attritor, their current circumstances then dictate whether or not they do in fact attrite—the "second hurdle."

The double hurdle model contains two equations.

$$d_i^* = z_i'\alpha + \varepsilon_i$$

$$y_i^{**} = x_i'\beta + u_i$$

$$\begin{pmatrix} \varepsilon_i \\ u_i \end{pmatrix} \sim N\left[\begin{pmatrix} 0 \\ 0 \end{pmatrix}, \begin{pmatrix} 1 & 0 \\ 0 & \sigma^2 \end{pmatrix}\right]$$

The first hurdle is then represented by:

$$d_i = 1 \text{ if } d_i^* \geq 0$$

$$d_i = 0$$

$$\text{If } d_i^* \leq 0 \tag{7.4}$$

Equation 7.4 is therefore close to a probit representation. The second hurdle closely resembles the Tobit Model.

$$y_i^* = \max\left(y_i^{**}, 0\right)$$

Finally, the observed variable y_i is determined as follows:

$$P_{\text{ET}} = d_i y_i^*$$

where P_{ET} is the probability of early termination.

The log-likelihood function for the double hurdle is as follows:

$$\text{Log}L = \sum_0 \text{In}\left[1 - \Phi(z_i'\alpha)\Phi\left(\frac{x_i'\beta}{\sigma}\right)\right] + \sum_+ \text{In}\left[\Phi(z_i'\alpha)\frac{1}{\sigma}\varphi\left(\frac{y_i - x_i'\beta}{\sigma}\right)\right]$$

Loss Model—Double Hurdle Approach

A similar approach has been adapted to model the loss and balance at risk due to default. The objective is to identify those customers who will possibly default and target them based on their balance at risk (B@R). The "first hurdle" is whether the customer is a potential defaulter. Given that the borrower is a potential defaulter, the "second hurdle" is the balance at risk (B@R) of the defaulter.

As shown above, the double hurdle model contains two equations.

$$h_i^* = y_i'\delta + \varepsilon_i$$

h_i^* = 1, if consumer is a potential defaulter then "1";

Else "0"

$$b_i^{**} = w_i'\gamma + u_i$$

$$b_i^{**} = \text{Balance at Risk (B@R)}$$

$$b_i = \max(b_i^{**}, 0)$$

Finally, the observed variable y_i is determined as follows:

$$B@R = h_i b_i$$

We use the log likelihood similar to the attrition model scenario as shown above.

7.3.4 CRM Through Cross-Sell and Up-Sell

One of the keys to success in the consumer finance business is the ability to convert the short-term customer relationships into long-term relationships through effective CRM. This can be achieved through cross-sell and up-sell of products to the customers. Therefore, the pricing solution should not only take into account the specific product profitability but also the customer lifetime profitability by considering opportunities of cross-sell and up-sell. However, an effective cross-sell and up-sell strategy requires a good understanding of different classes of customers and the possible opportunities to market different products, line extensions, and new product categories. It is also important to understand the customers' propensity to respond to various offers and the best time to make the right offers. This chapter thus proposes a simple logistic regression model for capturing the customers' propensity to respond to various cross-sell and up-sell programs.

7.3.5 Segmentation

The price differentiation as an ability to charge differentiated price is often used as a method of augmenting business profit. The price differentiation in consumer finance business would typically involve charging a different price to different segments of customers based on their willingness to pay, risk, and profitability of various segments. Therefore, one of the objectives of the proposed price optimization solution is to divide the market into various segments, such that a differentiated price can be charged based on the factors mentioned above.

Typically, many of the existing pricing solutions take the business pricing rules as the domain of price optimization. However, in contrast, this chapter introduces advanced clustering technique to divide customers into meaningful segments and use these clusters as domain of optimization. Cluster analysis provides techniques to discover structure (segments) within a given set of data where the homogeneity among customers in a cluster is minimized, while the heterogeneity across clusters is maximized. Though there are several clustering techniques available such as hierarchical, K-means, Fuzzy-c-means, and genetic algorithm-based cluster, this chapter proposes a sophisticated segmentation technique based on "genetic algorithm," as it provides one of the most efficient and effective techniques for segmentation.

7.4 Segmentation Through GA

Since the superiority of the GA clustering over the commonly used K-means is well documented, we propose a GA-based clustering for this chapter. The searching capability of GA is used to locate cluster centers such that a similarity metric of these resulting clusters is optimized. Furthermore, the GA-based cluster scores higher than the traditional techniques since most of the traditional clustering techniques do not provide the optimal number of clusters in a data set. Therefore, GA-based cluster solutions not only offer the optimal number of clusters in a data set but also is capable of efficiently and automatically forming natural groups using an unsupervised learning by means of an evolutionary approach.

A typical process of GA-based clustering is shown in Fig. 7.4.

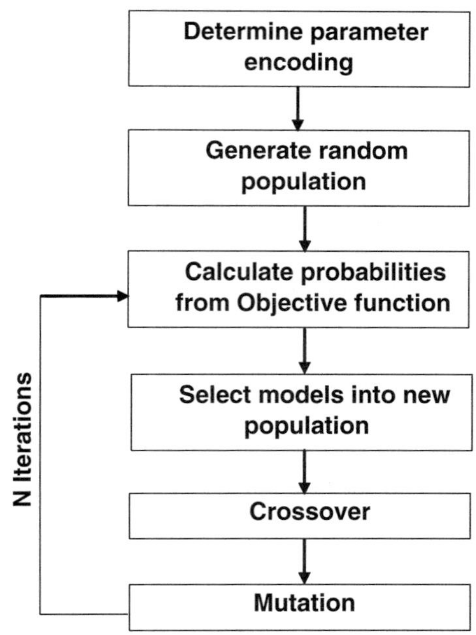

Fig. 7.4 Typical GA process steps

7.4.1 Optimization—Local Versus Global Optimum

In contrast to most optimization problems, where the goal is to achieve the global optimum, the price optimization proposed in this chapter seeks to attain a local optimum in the neighborhood of the existing pricing practice, thereby ensuring that there are no drastic deviations of proposed pricing from the current pricing. The local optimum, as opposed to global optimum which often suggests a significant change in the price, is preferred since the smaller incremental changes in price makes it much more acceptable to the business for implementation.

7.4.2 Regulatory Constraints, Market Dynamics, and Competitive Conquest

Since most of the consumer finance businesses operate in a regulated environment, one of key requirements of the pricing solution would be to incorporate these constraints while searching for the optimal price solution. The pricing framework developed in this chapter allows incorporating these considerations through a constrained optimization setting where the constraints such as maximum and minimum price charged to different segments can be invoked while deriving the optimal solution.

Similarly, the market dynamics is another important factor that needs to be considered while developing an optimal pricing. For example, cost of capital, the mortgage, and home equity rates change very often, and hence, in order to accurately determine optimal prices for various market segments, price optimization solution should be able to recalibrate the prices and take into account the changes in economic conditions, consumer behavior, and competitive actions.

7.5 The Optimization Model

The final price optimization framework is obtained by combining the key components specified above. The objective here is to maximize the total net revenue (TNR) by incorporating the various components subject to the specific constraints as defined by the life cycle of a customer (Fig. 7.5). The three key components of TNR are the revenue (R), cost (C), and loss (L). In simple terms, this can be represented as follows:

$$\text{TNR} = \text{R} - \text{C} - \text{L}$$

The revenue component relies on income earned through cross-sell and up-sell, adjusted by price elasticities and early termination propensity, while the cost

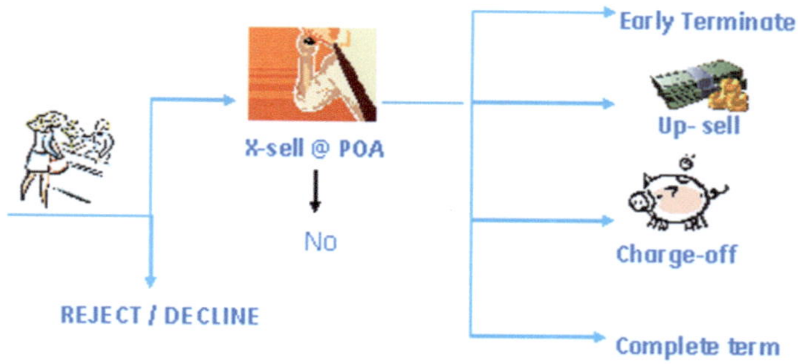

Fig. 7.5 Customer life cycle map

component is determined based on the net debt on books. The loss component consists of loss due to delinquency and charge-offs.

A typical optimization framework can thus be represented as follows:

$$\begin{aligned}\text{TNR} = \lambda(r)\{[P_{\text{ET}}(r * \text{Rev}_{\text{ET}}) + (1 - P_{\text{ET}})(r * \text{Rev}_{\text{FT}})] + P_{\text{x}s}(\text{Rev}_{\text{X-sell}}) \\ + P_{\text{up}}(\text{Rev}_{\text{up-sell}}) - (CF) - l(r) * B@R(r)\}\end{aligned}$$

where Rev_{ET} is the revenue earned from the early terminated accounts; Rev_{FT} is the revenue earned from full term customers; $\text{Rev}_{\text{X-sell}}$ is the revenue earned through cross-selling; $\text{Rev}_{\text{up-sell}}$ is the revenue earned through an up-sell; P_{xs} is the likelihood of a cross-sell;

P_{up} is the likelihood of an up-sell; and CF is the cost of funds.

The optimization framework is as follows:

$$\underset{r_1, r_2 \ldots r_s}{\text{Max}} \ \text{TNR}$$

7.6 Simulation

This section presents the results of a simulation exercise carried out based on the proposed pricing framework. This simulation exercise presupposes the various model equations as given below.

Response model as:

$$\lambda(r)_i = \alpha - \beta r_i + u_i$$

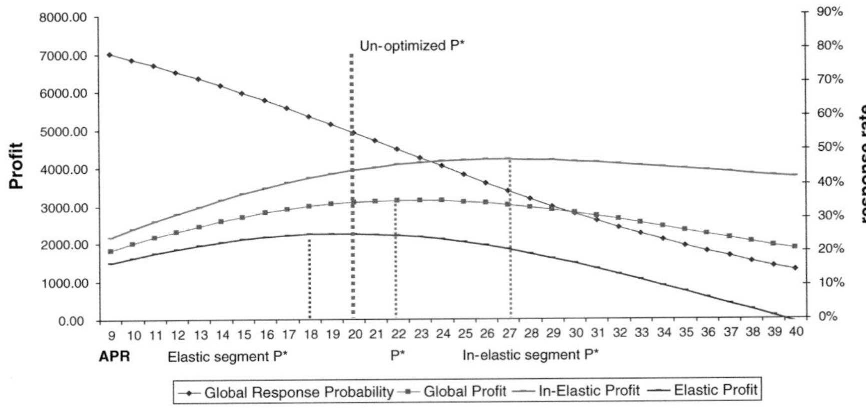

Fig. 7.6 Optimization framework: profit versus response

Early termination model as ET:

$$P_{\mathrm{ET}i} = \gamma + \delta r_i + u_i$$

Cross-sell model as:

$$P_{\mathrm{xs}i} = \phi - \mu r_i + u_i$$

Delinquency model as:

$$B@R_i = \varphi - \pi r_i + u_i$$

Figure 7.6 depicts the profit versus response graphs for the parameter values:

$\alpha = 2.2135,\ \beta = 0.1,\ \gamma = 0.1135,\ \delta = 0.031,\ \phi = 0.1535,\ \mu = 0.021,\ \varphi = 0.0135$ and $\pi = 0.171$

In the above construct, the optimum price for the entire market is 23 %, since any increase in price beyond this point would result in a decline in the profit. The point where the profit is maximized (approximately at $3000) is the optimum price. The graph illustrates the possibility of charging a differentiated price depending on the elasticities of each individual segment. Typically for a low elastic segment, the optimum price would be higher than the global optimum, as seen in this case at approximately 27 %, while for the high elastic segment, the optimum as 18 %.

7.7 Summary

This chapter develops a robust price optimization framework by considering not only the short-term gain maximization but also the long-term gain by incorporating the various components of a customer life cycle. The significant contribution of this chapter involves developing a framework that explicitly and transparently takes into account the price response and adverse elasticity concepts. Also in order to successfully capture the consumer behavior, this chapter introduces advanced modeling techniques such as the double hurdle model, in contrast to the more traditional logistic models, and demonstrates its efficiency to model attrition and risk. Additionally, this chapter introduces a sophisticated clustering technique called "genetic algorithm" for segmentation analysis. Finally, this chapter presents the results from a simulation study to provide an insight into the key benefits of this framework. With further research, the true power of the proposed framework's applications in different portfolios can be recognized.

References

Agrawal V, Ferguson M (2006) Optimal customized pricing in competitive settings. Working Chapter

Cragg JG (1971) Some statistical models for limited dependent variables with application to the demand for durable goods. Econometrica 39(5):829–844

Friedman L (1956) A competitive-bidding strategy. Oper Res 4:104–112

Gates M (1967) Bidding strategies and probabilities. J Constr Div 93:75–103

Gupta S, Lehmann D, Stuart J (2004) Valuing customers. J Mark Res 41(1):7–18

King M, Mercer A (1991) Distributions in competitive bidding. J Oper Res Soc 42(2):151–155

Lawrence R (2003) A machine-learning approach to optimal bid-pricing. In: Proceedings of the eighth INFORMS computing society conference on optimization and computation in the network era, Chandler, Arizona

Lilien G, Kotler P, Moorthy KS (1992) Marketing models. Prentice Hall

Morin TL, Clough RH (1969) OPBID: competitive bidding strategy model. J Constr Div 85–106

Papaioannou V, Cassaigne N (2000) A critical analysis of bid pricing models and support tool. IEEE Int Conf Syst Man Cybernet 3:2098–2103

Phillips R (2005) Pricing and revenue optimization. Stanford Business Books

Yong C, Gruca TS (2005) Reducing adverse selection through customer relationship management. J Mark 69(4):219–229

Chapter 8
Customer Relationship Management (CRM) to Avoid Cannibalization: Analysis Through Spend Intensity Model

Saumitra N. Bhaduri, V. Anuradha, Avanti George and David Fogarty

Abstract The focus of the chapter is to model the cannibalization effect of a cobranded bank card upgrade program launched on Europe's retail cards data. Since most of the retail businesses operate in a non-contractual setting, differentiating between the customers who are loyal and those who will continue to maintain their in-store spends even after the upgrade is difficult. The chapter develops an in-store intensity model that challenges the conventional wisdom of building a model using a logistic or OLS regression technique. The methodology developed in this chapter clearly recognizes the existence of a group of potential customers who would direct all their spending on the out-of-store outlets and none on the in-store outlets, by identifying the "flipping point" of their intensities. The intensity model not only recognizes existence of this group of customer but also explicitly models the probability of actual purchase activity to depend on customer attributes, successfully demonstrating a significant improvement over the conventional technique by capturing the extent of in-store intensity and the selection criterion required to pinpoint the most profitable customers in a gainful manner. This methodology will certainly satisfy the retailers in terms of ensuring there is no drop in sales; however, further research is needed for looking beyond just maintaining in-store spend intensities on upgraded customers and optimizing the entire decision process across all of the key drivers of profitability in credit cards.

8.1 Introduction

With the onset of improved computing power along with an array of statistical tools to choose from, the face of CRM in consumer finance industry has changed radically. Statistical methods are now used in consumer finance business in many ways. They are almost used in all aspects of consumer behavior including creditworthiness, risk of default, risk of early repayment, probability of churn, probability of

---

This chapter contains contributions from V. Anuradha and Avanti George, Madras School of Economics, Chennai, India.

S.N. Bhaduri and D. Fogarty, *Advanced Business Analytics*,
DOI 10.1007/978-981-10-0727-9_8

declining an offered product, appropriateness for other products, fraud detection, pricing risk, improving the focus of mail shots, and segmentation.

Historically, such a phenomenal growth in sophisticated mathematical and statistical models can be attributed to the availability of huge amount of funding for analytics, the large number of companies using analytics (such as MBNA, GM, Capital One, People's Bank, and Bank one), and the need for refined models for increasingly competitive situations.

Traditionally, first-generation models have dominated the consumer analytics scenario. Typically, such consumer-scoring methods are aimed at identifying "good" and "bad" consumers according to their risk classes, their customer performance, their different behavior patterns, and in a wide verity of other ways.

Among other techniques, logistic regression has become the workhorse in consumer analytics. Albeit its simplicity and excellent prediction power for discrete events, logistic regression (and other similar classifier) has significant disadvantages. Therefore, though the first-generation models have served a significant value addition to businesses, they often pose a significant conceptual and implementation challenges. These models primarily focus on the "binary outcome" of an economic process, e.g., attrition, dormancy, payoff, or retention, and hence completely ignore the data generating process behind the consumer behavior.

However, recent years have seen a gradual recognition of this issue, which is succinctly captured by Hand (2001) as follows: "A further aspect of the choice of response arises when one takes into account the reasons for the customer falling into a given class. Take default on a loan as an example. Amongst those customers who default, some will do so because they set out to do so from the start (fraud), while others will do so because they experience economic difficulties (redundancy, marital breakdown). It seems inappropriate to seek to lump all these together under the general term "default" and hope to predict them all with a single rule with any accuracy. Rather, the fact that there are different kinds of default response should be acknowledged and different predictive rules built. This is hardly ever done" (Hand 2001).

The second-generation model proposed in this chapter attempts to capture such DGP (data generating process)-driven differential behavior. The proposed model has been developed to address one of the classic challenges of CRM analytics involving cannibalizing effect of a cobranded bank card upgrade. Specifically, this chapter develops a two-stage model to identify the in-store purchase intensity of customers after a card being upgraded to a cobranded bank card, which allows the customer to shop outside the issuing store. The primary objective of the model is to identify those customers who will continue to purchase in-store (i.e., within the retail network) and to what extent, even after being given the option to use the card out-of-store (i.e., outside of the retail network).

The chapter is organized as follows: Sect. 8.2 gives a brief overview of the two-stage model and discusses the methodology proposed in this chapter. Section 8.3 narrates the description of the data used. Section 8.4 provides the results. Section 8.5 is a brief comparison of the proposed two-stage model against the OLS technique. Finally, Sect. 8.6 concludes.

8.2 In-Store Purchase Intensity Model

The focus of this chapter is to model the cannibalization effect of a cobranded bank card program launched by one of Europe's foremost retail card company. The initial observation confirms a 5–10 % average decline in-store purchase in spite of overall spending being 20–30 % higher. Therefore, a successful cobranded bank card program would demand for a successful identification of loyal customers who will continue to maintain their in-store spends even after the upgrade. Retailers depend on private-label credit cards to generate incremental sales volume which can vary anywhere from 2 to 40 % of total annual sales volume. Therefore, they cannot afford to risk this income stream as issuers upgrade from PLCC to cobranded bank cards giving customers the opportunity to shop at competing retail outlets. In order to capture the loyal customers, a two-stage model have been developed where first stage captures a positive spend incident and the second stage ensures a higher in-store spend intensity.

The primary attraction of the framework is its ability to decompose the "zero intensity" customers based on their DGPs. The decomposition allows differentiating the dormant customer (no purchase) from only out-of-store customers, thereby suggesting differential CRM strategies for each of these groups.

Interesting to note that, many other studies have followed a similar structure of model in various aspects from estimating cigarette consumption (Jones 1989) to wildlife valuation (Espineira 2004). On the credit scoring front, Dionne et al. (1996) argued that estimating the default probabilities is not sufficient for appropriate evaluation of credit scoring and proposed a similar model. Moffat (2005) used a double hurdle model to estimate loan default.

8.2.1 Methodology

As the model name suggests, customers must cross two stages in order to complete a purchase process. The "first stage" needs to be crossed in order to be a spender, i.e., whether the customer makes a purchase or not. Given that the customer is a spender (i.e., he has made at least one purchase), the "second stage" captures the circumstances contributing to their intensity of in-store purchase.

8.2.2 In-Store Intensity Model

The Intensity model contains two equations.

$$d_i^* = z_i'\alpha + \varepsilon_i$$

$$y_i^{**} = x_i'\beta + u_i$$

$$\begin{pmatrix} \varepsilon_i \\ u_i \end{pmatrix} \sim N\left[\begin{pmatrix} 0 \\ 0 \end{pmatrix}, \begin{pmatrix} 1 & 0 \\ 0 & \sigma^2 \end{pmatrix}\right] \tag{8.1}$$

The diagonal of the covariance matrix indicates that the two error terms are independently distributed.

The first stage is then represented by:

$$d_i = 1 \text{ if } d_i^* > 0$$

$$d_i = 0 \text{ if } d_i^* \leq 0 \tag{8.2}$$

Equation (8.2) is, therefore, close to a Probit representation. The second stage closely resembles the Tobit model with the following specification.

$$y_i^{**} = x_i'\beta + u_i \qquad i = 1, \Lambda, n$$

$$u_i \sim N(0, \sigma^2)$$

where y_i^{**} is a latent variable representing the customer i's propensity to spend, x_i' is a vector of a customers characteristics relevant in explaining the extent of in-store intensity, β is a corresponding vector of parameters to be estimated, and u_i is a homoscedastic, normally distributed error term.

Let y_i be the actual in-store intensity. This chapter defines the customer's in-store intensity as the total in-store spend over the last 6 months, as a proportion of the total overall spend by the customer, over last 6 months, that is,

$$\text{In-Store Intensity} = \text{TIS/TS}$$

where TIS is the total in-store spend in last 6 months and TS is the total spend (both in-store and out-of-store) in last 6 months.

For example, if the customer spends all his money in-store, then his in-store intensity would be hundred percent, while conversely if he shifted completely to out-store spending, his in-store intensity would be zero. Since actual in-store intensity cannot be negative, the relationship between y_i^{**} and y_i is as follows:

$$y_i = \max(y_i^{**}, 0) \tag{8.3}$$

Equation (8.3) gives rise to the standard censored regression model widely known as Tobit model. The log-likelihood function for the Tobit model is as follows:

$$\text{Log}L = \sum_0 \text{In}\left[1 - \Phi\left(\frac{x_i'\beta}{\sigma}\right)\right] + \sum_+ \text{In}\left[\frac{1}{\sigma}\phi\left(\frac{y_i - x_i'\beta}{\sigma}\right)\right] \tag{8.4}$$

in which "0" indicates summation over the zero observations in the sample, while "+" indicates summation over positive observations. $\Phi(\cdot)$ and $\phi(\cdot)$ are the standard normal cdf and pdf, respectively.

Finally, the observed variable y_i is determined as follows:

$$\begin{aligned} y_i &= y_i^* \quad \text{if} \quad y_i^* > 0 \text{ and } d_i^* > 0 \\ y_i &= 0 \quad \text{otherwise} \end{aligned} \tag{8.5}$$

The log-likelihood function for the double hurdle is as follows:

$$\begin{aligned} \text{Log}L = &\sum_0 \text{In}\left[1 - \Phi(z_i'\alpha)\Phi\left(\frac{x_i'\beta}{\sigma}\right)\right] \\ &+ \sum_+ \text{In}\left[\Phi(z_i'\alpha)\frac{1}{\sigma}\phi\left(\frac{y_i - x_i'\beta}{\sigma}\right)\right] \end{aligned} \tag{8.6}$$

Maximum likelihood estimation is applied to estimate α and β jointly along with the σ.

8.2.3 Prediction

Estimating the predicted values of d_i* and y_i* is as important as estimating α and β.

From the estimated α coefficient, the probability of at least one purchase is calculated as follows:

$$d_i^* = \hat{p}(\text{activity}) = \Phi(z_i'\alpha).$$

The extent of in-store spend is calculated as follows:

$$y_i^{**} = \Phi(x_i'\beta/\sigma) * (x_i'\beta + \sigma * \left(\frac{\varphi(x_i'\beta/\sigma)}{\Phi(x_i'\beta/\sigma)}\right)$$

Finally, the expected in-store intensity is given as follows:

$$\hat{p}_i(\text{activity}) * y_i^{**}$$

8.2.4 Estimation

There is no standard routine available in SAS to estimate this in-store intensity model. The chapter estimates using the maximum likelihood routine PROC NLMIXED available in SAS.

8.3 Data

The data from Europe's foremost retail cards company have been used in this study. This retail data comprise of transaction records from June 2005 to June 2007. The observation window is taken from June 2005 to June 2006, while the next 6 months constitutes the performance window. The control group population comprised of customers who are not selected for any upgrade. The total number of observations is 105,556 of which the control group (population with no upgrade) accounts are 6876, which is 6 % of the population. Out of these 105,556 accounts, the control group was excluded for the study and the remaining 99,644 sampled accounts were further split into development and validation samples as 50:50. Final set of development sample has 47,649 observations and the validation sample with 47,649 observations.

The cannibalization of in-store spend is always been big concern for any upgrade program, and effective strategy to identify the intensity of in-store spend will hold the key to prevent it, through customized strategies.

8.3.1 Variables Used

The data consist of customer-level transaction information from June 2005 to June 2007. The dependent variables are created from the performance window, i.e., July 2006 to December 2006. For the model, an activity flag has been created, as the first stage-dependent variable. The flag takes the value of zero if the accounts do not have a single purchase and one otherwise.

We also compute an additional second stage-dependent variable, namely intensity of in-store purchase intensity as:

For the accounts that have at least one purchase, intensity is defined as follows:

$$\text{Intensity} = [\text{Total In-store spends/Total Overall spends}].$$

For all the non-active accounts, it by definition takes a value of zero. The selections of independent variables in the model are carried out after checking for correlation and multicollinearity. Finally, a robustness check has been performed for the proposed model using the validation sample.

8.4 Results

The estimates of the proposed model are presented in Table 8.1. The sample size used for the model development is 47,649.

Table 8.1 Model variables and their estimates

Variables	Description	Estimates	Probability
First hurdle			
Intercept	Intercept	0.1735	<0.0001
Max_n_txn_13	Maximum number of instore transaction in last 3 months	0.258	<0.0001
Rise_val_13	If average spend value in last 3 months is greater than the previous 3 months	−0.5694	<0.0001
d1_utilization	d1_utilization = (utilization <=0);	−0.08852	<0.0001
d2_utlization	d2_utilization = (0 < utilization <=0.01);	0.2937	<0.0001
d3_utilization	d3_utilization = (0.01 < utilization <=0.06);	0.2278	<0.0001
d4_utilization	D4_utilization = (0.06 < utilization <=0.18);	0.1284	<0.0001
d1_CREDIT_LIMIT	CREDIT_LIMIT <=1000	−0.0745	<0.0001
d2_CREDIT_LIMIT	(1000 < CREDIT_LIMIT <=2250);	0.1046	<0.0001
Intensity_Flag	If total_gross_spend in either of the last 3 months increased from its previous month	0.897	<0.0001
Increase_n_16	If average number of transaction in last 6 months is higher than that of first 6 months	−0.1143	<0.0001
Second hurdle			
Intercept	Intercept	0.8665	<0.0001
Intensity_flag	If total_gross_spend in either of the last 3 months increased from its previous month	0.03997	<0.0001
Increase_n_16	If average Number of transaction in last 6 months is higher than that of first 6 months	−0.01057	0.0019
utilization	BAL/CREDIT_LIMIT	−0.129	<0.0001
aax_n_txn_16	Maximum number of transactions in last 6 months	0.001379	<0.0001
avg_grosspent_13	Average spend value in last 3 months	−0.00011	0.0012
flag_max_n	If maximum frequency of transaction in last 3 months is higher than that of previous 3 months	−0.03068	<0.0001
SIGMA	Sigma	0.2763	<0.0001

All the variables included in the model are significant at 99.9 % level. Selection of variables is done through a routine multicollinearity check, having all VIFs less than 1.75. Focusing on the explanatory variables, such as utilization and trends in spend, seems to influence the first stage. It is interesting to note that the second stage is influenced additionally by the purchase frequency and recency explanatory variables (different dummies), thereby further justifying our choice of our two-stage intensity Model.

Table 8.2 shows the estimated in-store intensities, by the two-stage intensity model, vis a vis the actual in-store intensities. It interesting to note that the actual

Table 8.2 Predicted versus actual in-store intensities

Decile	freq	Avg_Actual_ Intensities	Avg_Estimated_ Intensities
1	4765	0.8985	0.9089
2	4765	0.8622	0.8744
3	4765	0.8409	0.8467
4	4765	0.8195	0.8129
5	4765	0.7766	0.7673
6	4765	0.7302	0.7034
7	4765	0.6206	0.5982
8	4765	0.4924	0.5297
9	4765	**0.4615**	**0.4676**
10	4765	0.4109	0.4350

Flip from in-store activity to out-store activity

Table 8.3 Percentage of spends captured

8th decile	Development sample (%)	Validation sample (%)
% of total spend captured up to 8th decile	83	83
% of total internal spend captured up to 8th decile	86	87
% of total external spend captured up to 8th decile	77	75
% of total accounts captured up to 8th decile	70	70

Table 8.4 Average spends of selected population versus control group intensities of all numbers are in local currency

Population	Average internal spends	Average external spends	Average total spends
Development sample (selected population only)	354	174	472
Validation sample (selected population only)	352	175	473
Control group	326	0[a]	326

[a]NA by definition

flip from in-store to out-store purchase occurs in the 9th decile. This implies that up to the 8th decile, on an average, the customers have a higher tendency to spend within the retail stores than on external purchases, thereby justified for being selected for the upgrade program.

The percentage of spends captured up to the 8th decile is shown in Table 8.3. A comparison of the development sample with the validation sample shows that the model is stable, since the performance is analogous. Table 8.4 shows the average spends of the selected population versus the control group.

The selected population has higher average in-store spends than the control group. Since there is no upgrade given to control population, there is zero external spends. Thus, by scoring people using the proposed two-stage model and selecting the population up to the 8th decile, we are able to capture those customers who do not shift their spend to out-of-store outlets, but will, however, remain loyal and retain their spending in the in-store retail outlets.

8.5 Beyond Conventional Intensity Model

This section compares the strategy of using a conventional logistic or OLS model with an intensity model proposed in this chapter.

The conventional wisdom of developing a selection model to estimate the probability of whether or not a customer needs to be selected for upgrade (i.e., yes or no) is done by using a logistic regression. And the customary technique of developing an intensity model, to estimate the in-store intensities of customers, is done by using the OLS techniques. However, in this particular scenario, the focus of analysis is on the additional aspect of whether or not a customer with upgrade will shift his spend to the out-of-store retail. Since we are interested in distinguishing the dormant customers (no purchase) from only out-of-store customers (those whose purchases are solely out-of-store), we developed an intensity model in which the purchase activity probability is estimated using a Probit model and in-store intensity has been estimated using a Tobit Model.

As mentioned in the methodology, the expected in-store intensity is given as follows:

$$\text{P (Spend Active)} * \text{Predicted (In-store Intensity)}$$

Table 8.5 gives all possible outcomes decomposed by using the intensity model.

As shown in Table 8.5, there are two different possible outcomes for the "zero" in-store intensity observations. Using the intensity model, we are able to distinguish between those customers with upgrade who will shift their spend to the out-of-store retail versus those who retain their loyalty.

Therefore, the proposed method differentiates itself from the conventional logistic model, which would be able to identify customer for upgrade discretely

Table 8.5 Scenario from the intensity model

Spend active ($\hat{p}_i$(activity))	In-store intensity ($\hat{y}$)	
	Low	High
Low	In-store and out-store inactive	In-store and out-store inactive
High	In-store and out-store active	Active

based on a limited set of independent variables or from the traditional OLS which would only be able to identify people who are in-store inactive versus in-store active, by its ability to decompose the DGP of purchase behavior of the customers, both in-store as well as out-of-store.

8.6 Conclusion

The chapter develops an in-store intensity model that challenges the conventional wisdom of building a model using a logistic or OLS regression technique. The methodology developed in this chapter clearly recognizes the existence of a group of potential customers who would direct all their spending on the out-of-store outlets and none on the in-store outlets.

Most importantly, the intensity model not only recognizes existence of this group of customer but also explicitly models the probability of actual purchase activity to depend on customer attributes. Finally, the model successfully demonstrates a significant improvement over the conventional technique by capturing the extent of in-store intensity and the selection criterion required to pinpoint the most profitable customers in a gainful manner. This chapter makes a significant original contribution in terms of outlining an effective quantitative methodology to aid in the decision-making process for cobranded bank card upgrades. This methodology will certainly satisfy the retailers in terms of ensuring there is no drop in sales; however, further research is needed for looking beyond just maintaining in-store spend intensities on upgraded customers and optimizing the entire decision process across all of the key drivers of profitability in credit cards. For instance, cobranded bank cards typically have lower interest rates than single-purpose private-label credit cards. This variation varies anywhere from 500 to 1000 basis points. Therefore, the decision on whether to upgrade a customer from a private-label credit card to a cobranded bank card should also depend on a lift in overall spend to compensate for the drop in yield associated with the transfer if the customers maintained the existing level of spend. However, the challenge here is how much the customer can really spend in-store, especially if the retailer is not a general merchandiser and their products are very focused within a certain category (e.g., health and beauty aides). In this case, the optimal situation would be to maximize the in-store spend and out-of-store spend in non-competing retailers. On the last scenario, an example would be a health and beauty retailer encouraging out-of-store sales in a home improvement store. While the results of this chapter suggest that exploring the modeling of these more complex scenarios would be fruitful, it is beyond the scope of this study and is therefore a suggestion for further research.

References

Dionne G, Artis M, Guillen M (1996) Count data models for a credit scoring system. J Empir Finance 3(3):303–325

Espineira RM (2004) A box-cox double-hurdle model of wildlife valuation: the citizen's perspective. In: Chapter presented on the sixth annual BIOECON conference held at Kings College Cambridge, 2–3 Sept 2004

Hand DJ, Mannila H, and Smyth P (2001) Principles of data mining. MIT Press

Jones A (1989) A double-hurdle model of cigarette consumption. J Appl Econometrics 4(1):23–39

Moffat P (2005) Hurdle models of loan default. J Oper Res Soc 56:1063–1071

Chapter 9
Estimating Price Elasticity with Sparse Data: A Bayesian Approach

David Fogarty and Saumitra N. Bhaduri

Abstract Missing values and sparse data often challenge the reliability of statistical analysis in terms of biased parameter estimates and degraded confidence intervals, thereby leading to false inferences and suboptimal business decisions. To managers in the consumer data analytics field, the challenge faced by missing and limited data is nothing novel, and many powerful techniques of analysis and data management are available to them. However, the choice of adequate management practices is far from optimal. This chapter proposes an integrated approach by jointly treating the missing data and sparse data problems, using approximate Bayesian bootstrap (ABB) and Bayesian (HB) modeling. Therefore, the chapter addresses these two key challenges and corrects the bias formed, by extrapolating information from the sparse and missing data onto a large sample. The proposed method is illustrated by computation of price elasticity models for a leading consumer finance business on data that suffers from both missing and sparsity issues. The results presented illustrate the superiority of the model in taking better decisions in consumer data analytics. In contrast to the point estimate generated using traditional price elasticity models, the proposed model helps to make a better inference on the price elasticity estimates through a probability density function as it generates a distribution of price elasticity. Further expansion of the principle illustrated here will auger a powerful business optimization possibility and should be a fruitful area of future research.

9.1 Introduction

With the onset of improved computing power along with an array of statistical tools to choose from, the face of customer relationship management (CRM) in the consumer finance industry has changed radically. However, the successful implementation of these statistical methods requires handling of two important challenges encountered in the analysis of customer data in the form of missing values and sparse data. There is dearth of literature which addresses missing values and sparse data problem in consumer finance business. Hence, the central aim of this chapter is to develop a unified framework which examines missing values and sparse data problem specifically in consumer finance businesses.

S.N. Bhaduri and D. Fogarty, *Advanced Business Analytics*,
DOI 10.1007/978-981-10-0727-9_9

Missing values, by and large, complicate the statistical analysis in terms of biased parameter estimates, reduced statistical power, and degraded confidence intervals and thereby may lead to false inferences (Little and Rubin 1987). Similarly, sparse data accentuates the negative impact of outliers in the data set and is also susceptible to the violation of the assumptions underlying the estimated models. Therefore, determining an appropriate analytical strategy which takes care of challenges arising from both the sparse data and the missing data is imperative for consumer finance business. The primary objective of this chapter is to use Bayesian models to address the sparse and missing data issues and, to our knowledge, is the first attempt made with respect to the use of an integrated approach, in a consumer finance business.

The principle contribution of this chapter is twofold. First, it uses the approximate Bayesian bootstrap (ABB), form of imputation-based procedure, for dealing with missing values in consumer loan business. It also develops a Bayesian framework for dealing with sparse data. This chapter proposes a new method for treating missing data and sparse data problems jointly, using models developed through ABB and Bayesian modeling. Second tests the efficacy of Bayesian models over traditional techniques such as logistic regression in developing price elasticity models for consumer finance business. The technique developed in this chapter is applied to an existing price optimization solution (in Enabling Incremental Gains through Customized Price Optimization, Bhaduri et al.) that helps businesses improve their margins and increase volumes. The solution incorporates all of the features of modern commercially available pricing optimization solutions. It analyzes the price response elasticities and adverse selection elasticities that are crucial features of the pricing framework. However, the elasticities that are used conventionally are point estimates and often suffer due to limitations of sparse data and missing data. In contrast to the point elasticity, the method proposed in this chapter allows us to incorporate the pricing information and thereby generates a distribution of elasticity so that inference can be more reliably.

The rest of the chapter is organized as follows. The next section briefly reviews the existing literature. Section 9.3 describes the methodology employed. Section 9.4 reports and discusses the results obtained, and conclusion is given in the last section.

9.2 Methodology

9.2.1 Methodology for Missing Value Techniques

The literature on the missing data techniques (MDTs) has flourished since the early 1970s spurred by advances in computer technology that made previously laborious numerical calculations a simple matter. In the late 1970s, Dempster et al. (1977) formalized the EM (expectation maximization) algorithm, a computational method for efficient estimation from incomplete data. Until that time, missing data were viewed as a nuisance to be gotten rid of, either by case deletion of mean imputation. Since then, statisticians have realized that in any complete data set, the observed values provide indirect evidence about the likely value of unobserved ones. This evidence, when combined with certain assumptions, implies a predictive probability distribution for the missing values that should be averaged over in the statistical analysis (Schafer and Olsen 1998). In comparison with the development of traditional statistical methods, the literature on the analysis of partially missing data is relatively recent; review chapters include Afifi and Elashoff (1966), Hartley and Hocking (1971), Orchard and Woodbury (1972), Dempster et al. (1977), and Little (1982).

Methods proposed in the previous chapters can be clustered into four non-mutually exclusive categories. The first category of procedures proposed in the literature review is based on the complete-case procedures. In these procedures, when some variables are not recorded for some of the units, the method is to discard them and analyze only the units with complete data (e.g., Nie et al. 1975). This strategy may be satisfactory with small amounts of missing data and, however, can lead to serious biases. The second category of MDTs is known as available-case procedures. Pairwise deletion is a member of this category and works by deleting information only from those statistics that "need" the information. The disadvantage of using these procedures is that the sample base varies from variable to variable according to the pattern of missing data and loss of statistical power (Little and Rubin 1987). The third category of methods is referred to as weighting procedures. In this method, randomization inferences from sample survey data with non-response are commonly based on design weights, which are inversely proportional to the probability of selection. The fourth category of methods is referred to as imputation-based procedures. Data imputation refers to methods that impute the values of items that are missing. Roth (1994) reported that imputation-based procedures have a number of advantages. First, imputation strategies save a great deal of information since no individual is deleted from the analysis. Furthermore, the imputed data preserve deviation from the mean and the shape of the distribution. The main methods of imputation include mean imputation, hot deck imputation, cold deck imputation, regression imputation, stochastic regression imputation, composite methods, maximum likelihood, EM, and multiple imputations (Little and Rubin 1987; Efron and Tibshirani 1993; Roth 1994; Rubin 1996; Hedeker and Gibbons 1997).

In this chapter, in order to resolve the missing value challenge, a multiple imputation approach known as the approximate Bayesian bootstrap approach is employed. This approach to the multiple imputation of missing data uses the approximate Bayesian bootstrap to draw ignorable repeated imputations from the posterior predictive distribution of the missing data stratified by a propensity score for the observed versus the missing data.

The task of using an imputation approach to facilitate the statistical matching begins with a temporary variable which is created and is used as the dependent variable in a propensity model. The temporary variable will equal 0 for every case where the target variable is missing and will equal 1 otherwise. The independent variables for the model are a set of baseline/fixed covariates, which are thought to be related to the variable being imputed. Using the coefficients or weights, the propensity that a subject would not have been included in the data is calculated by the modeling of the missing values in the data set. In other words, this propensity score is the conditional probability of not being in the data set, given the vector of observed covariates. The statistical literature on matching methods such as the propensity score appears primarily in the context of observational studies for causal effects and the construction of control groups (Rosenbaum and Rubin 1983, 1985). The propensity score is defined in the literature under this context as the conditional probability of assignment to a particular treatment or group given a vector of observed covariates which can be used to match missing with observed customers for the purpose of imputation. Propensity score stratification was first suggested by Rosenbaum and Rubin (1983, 1985).

Propensity score stratification methods define a measure of distance "D0" between each missing and each observed customer, such as $(x' - x'')$ S-1 $(x' - x'')$t where x' and x'' refer to specific missing and observed values of Xi, and S is the covariance matrix of Xi in the observed sample. With multiple imputations, the matching observed customer for a missing could be the closest observed customers, or those supplemented with all those observed, less than some fixed distance "D0" away from the missing customer. Thus, each missing customer will have available, matching observed customers, to which the approximate Bayesian bootstrap method could then be applied to extract multiple imputations.

The objective is to estimate the difference in overall customer behavior between the observed and missing observations. In order to introduce the concept of matching based on the balancing score, the sampling distribution of the observed customers must be considered. Therefore, let the conditional probability of assignment to the observed population be given the covariates, as denoted by:

$$\rho(x) = \text{pr}\,(z = 1 \mid x),$$

The function $\rho(x)$ is the propensity score. The propensity score is the inclination toward being complete on a given attribute, given the observed covariates. In this chapter, it is seen that advanced techniques such genetic algorithms (GAs) can in some cases be superior for the linking attitudinal segments to behavioral databases. A brief description of the GA, as used to develop the propensity scores, is given below.

GAs are used to develop propensity scores to optimize a given objective function. A group of procedures is therefore created to implement a genetic algorithm. Initially, several potential solutions are randomly generated to form the initial population. A "solution" to the problem to be solved is represented by a list of alphanumeric characters, called a chromosome. The user of the algorithm may seed the gene pool with "hints" to form an initial population of possible solutions. For example, an existing scorecard can be used to seed this initial population. During each successive generation, each individual is evaluated by a numerical "fitness." The next step is to generate a second-generation population of chromosomes, based on the processes of selection and meiotic reproduction of selected individuals through the pseudo-genetic operators of "crossover" and "mutation." For each new individual to be produced, a pair of parent solutions is selected for "breeding." Selection is biased so that better solutions are more likely to be selected, but not guaranteed to be selected. Following selection, the crossover operation is performed upon selected chromosomes. Commonly, genetic algorithms have a probability of crossover, between 0.6 and 1.0, which denotes the probability that two selected parental chromosomes will generate offspring which differ from the parent solutions via mimicry of genetic recombination. These offspring are then added to the "next"-generation population.

The next step is to "mutate" the newly created offspring. Typical genetic algorithms have a fixed probability of mutation on the order of 0.01 or less. These processes ultimately result in the next-generation population of chromosomes that is different from the initial generation. Generally, the average fitness will have increased by this procedure for the population, since only the best organisms from the first generation are selected for breeding. The entire process is repeated for this second generation: Each organism is evaluated, the fitness value for each organism is obtained, pairs are selected for breeding, a third-generation population is generated, etc. This process is repeated until a termination condition has been reached which could be in the form of fixed number of generations being reached or allocated budget being reached among others.

There is a very wide literature on GAs, including explanations of varying clarity on why these algorithms work efficiently and effectively (Goldberg 1989; Spector et al. 1998 and Mitchell 1998). For our purposes, GA represents an extremely convenient class of search algorithms for propensity scoring for statistical matching. The use of a GA for estimating the propensity score "$\rho(x)$" in the approximate Bayesian bootstrap multiple imputations algorithm will represent the first multiple imputations application using genetic algorithms in the existing literature.

Next, the data are divided into groups based on quintiles of the propensity score. Quintiles are a set of four values, which divide the total frequency of a variable into five equal parts. Within each quintile, the number of observed and missing values of the target variable is counted. Next, a random sample is drawn with replacement, from the observed responses in the propensity quintile, equal in size to the number of observed data. This creates a posterior predictive distribution of the variable of interest. A second random sample is then drawn, with replacement, equal in size to the number of missing values in the quintile, and this second random sample is then used to fill in the missing values.

This whole process is repeated 5 times so that the result is 5 complete data sets, where the multiple imputations are independent repetitions from the posterior predictive distribution of interest. The choice to repeat the process 5 times is based on Schafer and Olsen (1998) who show that multiple imputations can be highly efficient for even small values. It has been observed that for a normal total percentage of missing data in a field, the gains from multiple imputations diminish rapidly after the first few imputations. Therefore, in many applications, just 3–5 imputations are sufficient to obtain excellent results.

9.2.2 *Methodology for Sparse Data Techniques*

Quantitative analysis in consumer data analytics hinges on models which are often faced with challenges stemming from sparse data. These models are used for forecasting and planning and therefore frequently require sizeable historical data, to obtain the future forecasts. However, ample data are not always easily available in the industry. Due to this data requirement, early forecasts are not viable, using traditional models. For example, a model may relate the future sales to the current marketing activity in the business. Estimates of these parameters are required to plan the level of marketing effort and to project potential sales. With the use of traditional methods, substantial amounts of sales and marketing history data are necessary to be observed, before the model parameters are readily estimated by maximum likelihood or weighted least squares. Bayesian methods can be effectively used to obtain early forecasts, by modeling parameters from previously existing cases or from smaller data, and these initial parameter estimates can be updated as and when the data become available. Bayesian models use prior beliefs and transform it into a statistic so that inferences can be made about the customers. The prior distribution also allows the ability to incorporate the knowledge or experience of the manager by augmenting a likely range of values of the parameters into the analysis. As sales data become available for the product, this prior distribution is updated by Bayes theorem, and the forecasts adapt to the unique features of the product.

One way to obtain the initial estimates is to pool the data from previous, relevant cases. Claycamp and Liddy (1969) took this approach in predicting new product performance. Another common method is to use averages or other statistical summaries (norms) of the estimates from previous cases as estimates for the parameters in the current case. A natural extension of these approaches is to use the estimates together with their distributions as priors in a Bayesian regression model. For example, Lilien et al. (1981) used this approach to predict the sales of a new ethical drug that is similar to a previously modeled drug. The parameters are updated using Bayesian regression, which provides a way to obtain early forecasts while at the same time adapting to the unique features of the case.[1] In the absence of any prior study, Bayesian estimation also allows us to integrate into the analysis, the view of the manager's beliefs which is extremely vital to any consumer finance business.

The hierarchical Bayesian (HB) methods offer another alternative approach and have a wide variety of applications in data analytics. The work by Lenk and Rao (1989)

---

[1] All these approaches assume that the variation in the estimates of the common parameter is due to sampling variation. This is the statistical justification of the Claycamp and Liddy approach; Lilien, Rao, and Kalish do the same thing by their restriction to "similar products." In many cases, however, data to support this assumption are not available, or similar products, with respect to sales rates, are hard to identify. For example, the parameters of marketing effectiveness may be functions of product characteristics. Rao and Yamada (1988) have studied the situation when the parameters are functions of perceived product attributes; see also Srivastava et al. (1985), Sultan et al. (1996), steckel and Vanhonacker (1988) and Batra and Vanhonacker (1988) for methods of using past cases for forecasting the diffusion of new products.

re-emphasizes the importance and appropriateness of the Bayesian approach to solving marketing problems. Lenk and Rao's (1989) introduction to Bayes' (HB) procedures and their usefulness in early (and adaptive) forecasting are timely and appropriate. Neelamegham and Chintagunta (1999) have used a structure to forecast first-week sales of movies in international markets. Very recently, Talukdar et al. (2002) study diffusion of six products in a large number of industrialized and developing countries. Their work highlights the advantages of HB methodology in forecasting product sales, where the gains of the HB methods are greatest at the early stage of product introduction, when forecasts are often the most valuable.

The next section briefly illustrates a standard Bayesian model.

Consider a simple regression model described by a density $p(y/\theta)$ where θ is the parameter to be estimated from data:

$$y_t = \vartheta x_t + \epsilon_t; \quad \varepsilon_t \approx (\text{Normal}\,(0, \sigma^2)); \tag{9.1}$$

A probability distribution for θ is formulated as $\Pi(\theta)$, which is known as the prior distribution. The prior distribution expresses the beliefs, for example, on the mean, the spread, the skewness, and so forth, about the parameter. These beliefs about θ can be updated by combining information from the prior distribution and the likelihood, through the calculation of the posterior distribution, $p(\theta/y)$. The posterior distribution of the parameter θ is obtained using Bayes' theorem, which enables the combination of the prior distribution and the model in the following way:

$$p(y/\theta) = \frac{p(\theta/y)}{p(y)} = \frac{p(y/\theta)\Pi(\theta)}{p(y)} = \frac{p(y/\theta)\Pi(\theta)}{\int p(y/\theta)\Pi(\theta)d\theta} \tag{9.2}$$

The denominator

$$p(y) = \int p(y/\theta)\Pi(\theta)d\theta \tag{9.3}$$

is the normalizing constant of the posterior distribution. This quantity $p(y)$ is also the marginal distribution of y, and it is sometimes called the marginal distribution of the data. The likelihood function of θ is any function proportional to $p(y/\theta)$, that is, $L(\theta) \propto p(y/\theta)$.

From this, we can rewrite Eq. 9.2 as

$$p(\theta/y) = \frac{L(\theta)\Pi(\theta)}{\int L(\theta)\Pi(\theta)d\theta} \tag{9.4}$$

The marginal distribution $p(y)$ is an integral; therefore, as long as it is finite, the particular value of the integral does not provide any additional information about the posterior distribution. Hence, $p(\theta/y)$ can be written up to an arbitrary constant, presented here in proportional form as follows:

$$p(\theta/y) \propto L(\theta)\Pi(\theta) \tag{9.5}$$

i.e., posterior $\propto$ Likelihood$*$ priors

Simply put, Bayes' theorem allows the updation of existing knowledge with new information. The analysis starts with a prior belief $\Pi(\theta)$, and after learning information from data y, the belief on θ is updated and $p(\theta/y)$ is obtained. These are the essential elements of the Bayesian approach to data analysis.

While conceptually elegant, the Bayes' theorem involves calculations that are typically difficult to perform and require sophisticated computations. The emergence of the Markov chain Monte Carlo (MCMC) methods has eliminated this analytical bottleneck. Rather than deriving the analytic form of the posterior distribution, MCMC methods substitute calculations that, in effect, simulate draws from this distribution. Samples are generated from the posterior distribution, and these samples are used to estimate the quantities of interest. The freedom afforded by MCMC to explore the parameter space was one of the first exploited in the marketing literature (Allenby and Ginter 1995).

The MCMC method, as mentioned, is a general simulation method for sampling from posterior distributions and computing posterior quantities of interest. MCMC method draws samples successively from a target distribution, with each sample drawn depending on the previous one, hence the notion of the Markov chain. A Markov chain is a sequence of random variables, $\theta^1, \theta^2, \ldots$, for which the random variable θ^t depends on all previous θs only through its immediate predecessor θ^{t-1}. Markov chain applied to sampling can be considered as a mechanism that traverses randomly through a target distribution without having any memory of where it has been. Its next move is entirely dependent on where it is now.

9.3 Empirical Model

In this chapter, a Bayesian model is developed within the context of the price optimization solution. The primary objective is to enhance the pricing solution, which typically uses price elasticity as a key input to improve profits.

This price-response function is estimated using a typical maximum likelihood estimate of a general logit model, with *Yt* = 1, if the customer accepts the offer, else *Yt* = 0.

$$y_t = \begin{cases} 1 & \text{if} \quad \beta_0 + \beta_1 \,\text{price}_t + \beta_2 A_t + \varepsilon_t > 0 \\ 0 & \text{if} \quad \beta_0 + \beta_1 \,\text{price}_t + \beta_2 A_t + \varepsilon_t \leq 0 \end{cases} \quad \varepsilon_t \approx \text{Normal}\,(0, \sigma^2) \tag{9.6}$$

where A_t is a set of all other control variables.

A prior distribution is obtained from the probability density function of the price estimate, β_1, and the posterior distribution is subsequently computed.

An alternative specification of this model in the hierarchical framework can be written by introducing a latent variable z_t:

$$y_t = \begin{cases} 1 & \text{if} \quad z_t > 0 \\ 0 & \text{if} \quad z_t > 0 \end{cases}; \tag{9.7}$$

$$z_t = \beta_0 + \beta_1 \, \text{price}_t + \beta_2 A_t + \varepsilon_t \quad \varepsilon_t \approx \text{Normal}\,(0, \sigma^2) \tag{9.8}$$

The data from multiple respondents are modeled with Eqs. 9.7 and 9.8.

For the current analysis, the BGENMOD procedure in SAS in employed, which uses the Gibbs sampler, one of the many algorithms that Markov chain Monte Carlo (MCMC) methods comprise. A Gibbs chain for the posterior distribution is generated for the model parameters. The BGENMOD computes summary statistics (mean, standard deviation, quartiles, HPD and credible intervals, correlation matrix) and convergence diagnostics (autocorrelations; Geweke, and the effective sample size) for each parameter as well as the correlation matrix of the posterior sample. Trace plots, posterior density plots, and autocorrelation function plots that use ODS graphics are also provided for each parameter. These summary statistics will be discussed in detail in the result section.

9.4 Data

This chapter applies a model which is a combination of multiple imputation methods and Bayesian methods in a consumer finance business to resolve issues with data sets that are sparse and contain missing values. As mentioned in the introduction, the objective of this chapter is to enhance the pricing solution (Bhaduri et al.) which uses elasticity as a key input to boost margins and profits, through the use of the Bayesian techniques. The data which are from one of the largest consumer finance businesses have been used in this study. These data comprise of customer application information between October 2005 and March 2008 and the total number of observations in the data set is 35,565. Typically, the solution analyses the data by segmenting customers into homogenous groups based on their credit rating and the amount of loan volume they are offered. The credit rating is captured by a variable called "Credit_band," that takes values "AA", "A", "B", "C", "D", "E", and "FS", where "AA" signifies the highest credit quality while "FS" the lowest. The loan amount is a continuous variable, ranging from 3,000 to 50,000 in the local currency. This loan variable is further segmented into various bands of loan volume, on the basis of their distribution among customers, to create a "loan_band" variable. The entire data set is split into 56 smaller groups on the basis of these credit bands and loan bands. There are 7 credit bands obtained from the credit ranking and 8 loan bands from the loan amount. In order to make better pricing decisions for the business, price elasticity needs to be calculated for these

56 credit and loan band combinations. However, in certain categories, the number of observations is limited and furthermore contains missing values. To resolve these intricacies, the chapter employs a structure consisting of two steps. The first step is to treat missing value problem using the ABB multiple imputation techniques. The second step is to estimate price elasticity of a sparse data set using Bayesian methods. The results of these are presented below.

9.5 Results

This section presents the results for one subset data, of the 56 categories. The results are provided for category of data set where credit_band is "A" (i.e., fairly good credit rating) and loan_band is between 8,000 and 10,000. This segment suffers from being sparse as well as contains missing values. In the first step, the data set is treated for missing values using the ABB multiple imputation technique as described in detail above. Once all the missing values in the data set are matched, the second step is the calculation of the price elasticity distribution using the Bayesian method.[2]

In this analysis, the maximum likelihood estimates of the logistic regression parameters are taken as the independent priors and are employed as starting values for the simulation. Table 9.1 shows the priors for regression coefficients obtained from the logistic regression.

As mentioned, these estimates of the regression parameters are used as the priors for the Markov chain Monte Carlo (MCMC) simulation.

From the original sparse data set of 83 observations, a posterior sample with a size of 10,000 is generated through the Markov chain Monte Carlo (MCMC) simulation.

Inferences made from Bayesian based simulation need to be dealt with cautiously. There are usually two issues: First is to decide whether the Markov chain has reached its stationary or the desired posterior distribution, and second is to determine the number of iterations to keep after the Markov chain has reached stationarity. Convergence diagnostics help to resolve these issues.[3]

---

[2]This is done using the "PROC BGENMOD" procedure in SAS. In the PROC BGENMOD analysis, if no prior is specified by the user, a flat prior distribution is assumed on the regression coefficients which reflects ignorance of the location of the parameter, placing equal likelihood on all possible values the regression coefficient can take.

[3]It is important to note that many diagnostic tools are designed to verify a necessary but not sufficient condition for convergence. There are no conclusive tests that can tell you when the Markov chain has converged to its stationary distribution. Also, it is important to check the convergence of all parameters, and not just those of interest, before proceeding to make an inference. With some models, certain parameters can appear to have very good convergence behavior, but that could be misleading due to the slow convergence of other parameters.

Table 9.1 Regression coefficients obtained from the logistic regression

Analysis of maximum likelihood estimates					
Parameter	DF	Estimate	Standard error	Wald Chi-Square	Pr > ChiSq
Intercept	1	−1.0191	1.6113	0.4097	0.5221
APR (Price)	1	0.0002	0.0949	0.0163	0.8984
NMI1 (Net Monthly Income1)	1	−0.6682	0.6197	1.2060	0.2721
NMI2 (Net Monthly Income2)	1	−1.4414	0.8525	2.9074	0.0882
SEC (Secured)	1	0.8759	1.0332	0.6987	0.4032
PC1 (Professional Code1)	1	2.4605	0.9215	7.0580	0.0079
PC2 (Professional Code2)	1	1.0960	0.5691	3.6254	0.0569

Table 9.2 Geweke diagnostics

Geweke diagnostics		
Parameter	z	Pr > $\|z\|$
Intercept	0.104	0.927
APR (Price)	0.125	0.911
NMI1 (Net Monthly Income1)	0.685	0.501
NMI2 (Net Monthly Income2)	−0.981	0.321
SEC (secured)	−0.448	0.646
PC1 (Professional Code1)	0.569	0.578
PC2 (Professional Code2)	0.849	0.403

Table 9.3 Autocorrelations of the posterior samples

Autocorrelations of the posterior samples				
Parameter	Lag1	Lag5	Lag10	Lag50
Intercept	0.931	0.653	0.418	0.037
APR (Price)	0.940	0.675	0.432	0.032
NMI1 (Net Monthly Income1)	0.243	0.027	0.018	0.015
NMI2 (Net Monthly Income2)	0.096	0.006	0.026	0.002
SEC (secured)	0.852	0.423	0.166	−0.011
PC1 (Professional Code1)	0.128	0.036	0.006	0.019
PC2 (Professional Code2)	0.341	0.000	−0.013	0.023

As a default, the BGENMOD procedure computes three convergence diagnostics: the Geweke diagnostic (Table 9.2); the autocorrelations (Table 9.3); and the effective sample size (Table 9.4).

Geweke (1992) proposed a mean estimate convergence diagnostic for Markov chains based on a test for equality of the means of the first and last part of a Markov chain. If the samples are drawn from the stationary distribution of the chain, the two means are equal and Geweke's statistic has an asymptotically standard normal

Table 9.4 Effective sample size

Effective sample size			
Parameter	ESS	Correlation time	Efficiency
Intercept	455	22.69	0.06
APR (Price)	451	22.89	0.06
NMI1 (Net Monthly Income1)	5384	1.98	0.55
NMI2 (Net Monthly Income2)	7882	1.39	0.80
SEC (Secured)	988	10.37	0.11
PC1 (Professional Code1)	6886	1.58	0.70
PC2 (Professional Code2)	5014	2.12	0.51

distribution. This is a two-sided test based on a z-score statistic and large absolute z values signify rejection.

In Table 9.2, a low absolute value of "z" corresponding to the variable APR (i.e., price) indicates a good mixing.

The autocorrelation of the posterior samples is used as a diagnostic test, in which a high autocorrelations between long lags indicate poor mixing. In Table 9.3, it is observed that for all variables, autocorrelation is negligible after 50 lags which signify that mixing is fairly decent for all the variables. However, a better picture of variable mixing in Markov chains can be obtained after examining the remaining Geweke diagnostics, effective sample size (ESS), and the trace plots.

Another closely related measure of mixing is the effective sample size (ESS) (Kass et al. 1998).

ESS and correlation time are inversely proportional to each other, and low ESS or high correlation time indicates inappropriate mixing of the Markov chain.

In Table 9.4, for our model the relatively high ESS signifies a decent level of mixing of the variables.

In addition to the tests previously discussed, trace plots can be utilized as another diagnostic which provides a visual assessment of convergence. The trace indicates whether or not the chain has converged to its stationary distribution. It also conveys whether the chain is mixing well. The aspects of stationarity that are most recognizable from a trace plot are a relatively constant mean and variance. A chain that mixes well traverses its posterior space rapidly and it can jump from one remote region of the posterior to another in relatively few steps.

Therefore, trace plots for all the seven parameters in our model are shown in Fig. 9.1, and these indicate that the Markov chain of posterior samples has converged satisfactorily.

From the results of the tests shown above, there is no evidence to show non-convergence in our analysis.

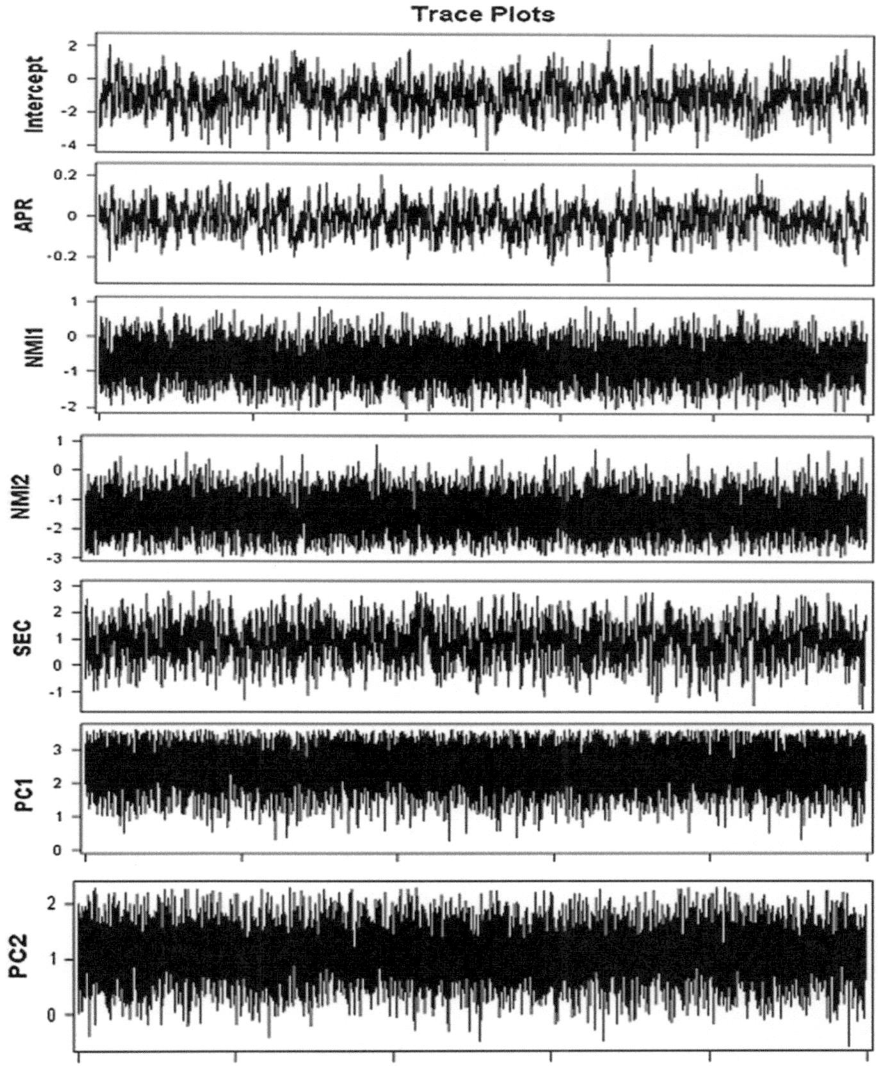

Fig. 9.1 Trace, autocorrelation, and density plot for Intercept

9.6 Distribution of Price Elasticities

Elasticity guides a percentage change in target variable (response) for a percentage change in input variable (price). Therefore, in our analysis, the price elasticity captures the percentage of change in response for a percentage change in price. Using traditional techniques, the elasticity of the sparse data set (with only 83 observations) is obtained at a single point, i.e., the point elasticity. This is done by employing the following formulas.

$$e_{\mathrm{APR}t} = \frac{\partial P(Y_t = 1|\mathrm{X}_t)}{\partial \mathrm{APR}_t} \bullet \frac{\mathrm{APR}_t}{P(Y_t = 1|\mathrm{X}_t)}$$

$$\frac{\partial P(Y_t = 1|\mathrm{X}_t)}{\partial \mathrm{APR}_t} = \text{scale} \bullet \beta_{APR} \quad \text{scale} = \frac{\exp(\mathrm{X}_t'\beta)}{[1 + \exp(\mathrm{X}_t'\beta)]^2}$$

$$e_{\mathrm{APR}t}\big|_{\text{mean}} = \frac{\hat{\beta}_{APR} A\bar{P}R}{[1 + \exp(\bar{\mathrm{X}}_t'\hat{\beta})]}$$

While using the above traditional logistic regression modeling technique formulas, a point elasticity of −0.090651 is obtained.

In contrast, the application of the Bayesian techniques as proposed in the chapter generates a distribution of elasticity as shown in Fig. 9.2.

Figure 9.1 shows the distribution of price elasticity obtained as the final result in contrast to the single point elasticity attained as a result of the traditional technique.

Table 9.5 below illustrates the descriptive statistics of price elasticity distribution.

The principle contribution of this method is the ability to generate a distribution of elasticity which is highly flexible when compared with the point estimate of elasticity that the traditional logistic regression generates. This range of elasticity helps the business gain an improved understanding and flexibility as far as the pricing is concerned. As seen from the descriptive statistics in Table 9.5, the mass of the elasticity distribution is negatively skewed at −0.160. The use of point estimates without acknowledging the amount of uncertainty will lead to overconfident predictions. This overconfidence can be avoided by using the Bayesian

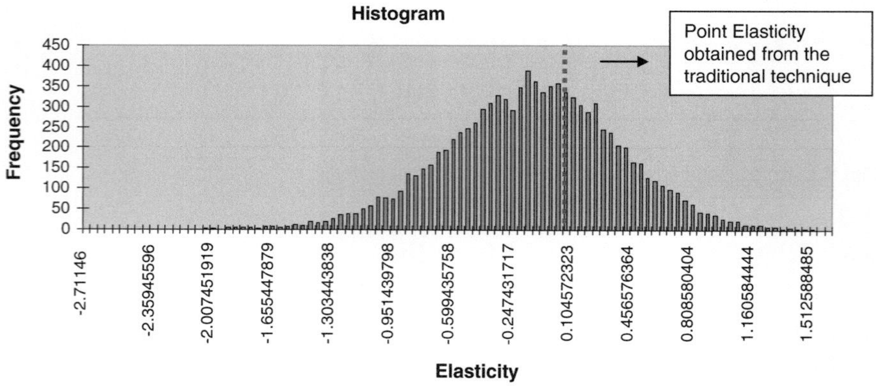

Fig. 9.2 Distribution of price elasticity

Table 9.5 Descriptive statistics of elasticity distribution

Descriptive statistics of elasticity distribution	
Mean	−0.102
Standard error	0.017
Median	−0.090
Mode	−0.183
Standard deviation	0.522
Sample variance	0.272
Kurtosis	0.252
Skewness	−0.148
Range	4.368
Minimum	−2.699
Maximum	1.657
Count	10000
Largest(1)	1.657
Smallest(1)	−2.699
Confidence level (95.0 %)	0.022

model which returns the distribution means, confidence intervals and also characterizes the uncertainty associated with predictions. In our analysis, the point estimate of −0.090651 generated by the traditional logistic technique appears as an overprediction of the elasticity when compared with the distribution of elasticity means, generated by the Bayesian model.

Therefore, from a consumer business manager's point of view, a distribution of elasticity using Bayesian methods is far superior to the point estimate of elasticity using traditional techniques. An elasticity distribution facilitates the manager getting a better understanding of how to price a consumer loan portfolio and it equips the manager in taking optimal pricing decisions by targeting the right set of customers. Additionally, it aids in the recognition of price bands for different customer segments and identifies the effect of these prices on the customer responses and consequently the profitability of the business. It further enhances the manager's bargaining power and enables effective customer management. Therefore, by means of the Bayesian technique, the fundamental objective of a typical consumer finance business, to "target the right segment of customers at the right price," is achieved by the manager.

9.7 Conclusion

The chapter makes a unique contribution by developing an integrated approach that addresses the key challenges of consumer finance business analytics with respect to missing values and sparse data. The results presented illustrate the superiority of the model in taking better decisions in consumer data analytics. In contrast to the point estimate generated using traditional price elasticity models, the proposed model helps to make a better inference on the price elasticity estimates through a probability density function as it generates a distribution of price elasticity.

To managers in the consumer data analytics field, the challenge faced by missing and limited data is nothing novel, and many powerful techniques of analysis and data management are available to them. However, the choice of adequate management practices is far from optimal. In this regard, the technique proposed in this chapter represents an integrated approach to resolve these two key challenges, thereby providing a useful decision-making engine that maps the data into profitable decisions. Further expansion of the principal illustrated here will auger a powerful business optimization possibility and should be a fruitful area of future research.

References

Afifi AA, Elashoff RM (1966) Missing observations in multivariate statistics I. J Am Stat Assoc 61 (315):595–605

Allenby GM, Ginter JL (1995) Using extremes to design products and segment markets. J Market Res 32:392–403

Batra R, Vanhonacker WR (1988) Falsifying laboratory results through field tests: a time-series methodology and some results. J Bus Res 16(4):281–300

Claycamp HJ, Liddy LE (1969) Prediction of new product performance: an analytical approach. J Market Res 6:414–420

Dempster AP, Laird LM, Rubin DB (1977) J Royal Stat Soc Seri B (Methodological) 39(1):1–38

Efron B, Tibshirani RJ (1993) An Introduction to the Bootstrap. Chapman & Hall, CRC Monographs on Statistics & Applied Probability

Geweke J (1992) Evaluating the accuracy of sampling-based approaches to the calculation of posterior moments. In: Bernardo JM, Berger JO, Dawid AP, Smith AFM (eds) Bayesian Statistics 4. pp 169–193. Oxford University Press, Oxford

Goldberg DE (1989) Genetic algorithms in search, optimization, and machine learning. TT Addison-Wesley Publishing Company Inc.

Hartley HO, Hocking RR (1971) The analysis of incomplete data. Biometrics 27:783–808

Hedeker D, Gibbons RD (1997) Application of random-effects pattern-mixture models for missing data in longitudinal studies. Psychol Methods 2(1):64–78

Lenk PJ, Rao AG (1990) New models from old: forecasting product adoption by hierarchical bayes procedures. Market Sci 9(1):42–53

Lilien G, Rao A, Kalish S (1981) Bayesian estimation and control of detailing effort in a repeat purchase diffusion environment. Manage Sci 27:493–506

Little RJA (1982) Models for nonresponse in sample surveys. J Am Stat Assoc 77:237–250

Little RJA, Rubin DB (1987) Statistical analysis with missing data. John Wiley and Sons, New York

Mitchell M (1998) An introduction to genetic algorithms. MIT Press, Cambridge, Massachusetts

Neelamegham R, Chintagunta P (1999) A Bayesian model to forecast new product performance in domestic and international markets. Market Sci 18(2):115–136

Nie NH, Hadlai CH, Jean GJ, Karin S, Bent DH (1975) Statistical package for the social sciences, 2nd edn. McGraw-Hill, New York

Orchard T, Woodbury MA (1972) A missing information principle: theory and applications. Proceedings of the 6th Berkeley Symposium on Mathematical Statistics and Probability, vol 1, pp 697–715

Rao AG, Yamada M (1988) Forecasting with a repeat purchase diffusion model. Manage Sci 34 (6):734–752

Rosenbaum PR, Rubin DB (1983) Assessing sensitivity to an unobserved binary covariate in an observational study with binary outcome. J Royal Stat Soc: Ser B 45:212–218

Rosenbaum PR, Rubin DB (1984) Reducing bias in observational studies using subclassification on the propensity score. J Am Stat Assoc 79:516–524

Rosenbaum PR, Rubin DB (1985) Constructing a control group using multivariate matched sampling methods that incorporate the propensity score. Am Stat 39:33–38

Roth PL (1994) Missing data: a conceptual review for applied psychologists. Pers Psychol 47 (3):537–560

Rubin DB (1996) Multiple imputation after 18+ years. J Am stat Assoc 91(434):437–489

Schafer JL, Olsen MK (1998) Multiple imputation for multivariate missing data problems: a data analyst's perspective. Multivar Behav Res 33:545–571

Spector L, Barnum H, Bernstein HJ (1998) Genetic programming for quantum computers. In: Koza JR, Banzhaf W, Chellapilla K, Deb K, Dorigo M, Fogel DB, Garzon MH, Goldberg DE, Iba H, Riolo RL (eds) Genetic Programming 1998: Proceedings of the Third Annual Conference, pp 365–374, Morgan Kaufmann

Srivastava RK, Mahajan V, Ramaswami SN, Cherian J (1985) A multi-attribute diffusion model for forecasting the adoption of investment alternatives for consumers. Technol Forecast Social Change 28(4):325–333

Steckel JH, Vanhonacker WR (1988) A heterogeneous conditional logit model of choice. J Bus Econ Stat 6(3):391–398

Sultan F, Farley JU, Lehmann DR (1996) Reflections on a meta-analysis of applications of diffusion models. J Market Res 247–249

Talukdar D, Sudhir K, Ainslie A (2002) Investigating new product diffusion across products and countries. Market Sci 21(1):97–114

Chapter 10
New Methods in Ant Colony Optimization Using Multiple Foraging Approach to Increase Stability

David Fogarty, Avanti George and Saumitra N. Bhaduri

Abstract With an ever-increasing need for firms to analyze data being collected from various sources such as the Internet and other forms of e-commerce, there is a greater need for more improved segmentation techniques for differentiated marketing programs aimed at maximizing revenues and profitability. K-means clustering is a popular technique for segmenting large data sets. Recently, algorithms mimicking the behavior of ant colonies have been shown to bring significant improvements to the K-means clustering algorithm and other methods of knowledge discovery in databases. These techniques were developed by imitating the behavior of real ants for finding the shortest path from their nests to the food source. This chapter represents an application that aims to cluster a data set by means of an ant colony optimization algorithm. It also increases the working performance of this algorithm used for solving the data clustering problem by proposing a multipronged foraging approach, resulting in the globally optimal solution and showing the advantage in the performance due to suggested technique. A limitation of this study is the generalizability of the results to other data sources as this algorithm was only tested in production on financial services data. Further research is necessary on additional sources of data from other domains.

10.1 Introduction

The majority of ant colony optimization problems focus on finding the shortest path using simulated behavior. The basic concept involves the fact that ants find the shortest path from their nest to a food source with the help of a pheromone trail. Ants communicate with one another by means of pheromone trails and exchanging information about which path should be followed. The more the number of ants that trace a given path, the more attractive this path (trail) becomes and is followed by other ants by depositing their own pheromone. Pheromone trails with higher

---

This chapter contains contributions from Avanti George, Madras School of Economics, Chennai, India.

S.N. Bhaduri and D. Fogarty, *Advanced Business Analytics*,
DOI 10.1007/978-981-10-0727-9_10

pheromone strength are preferred over others, while trails on the shorter paths increase more rapidly. These, among several others, are the unique characteristics of ants that are adapted on ant colony optimization algorithms to solve optimization problems.

Building upon the seminal works authored by Dorigo et al. (1996, 1999), many researchers have observed additional ant behavior in both experimental and natural settings: Some are Peters et al. (2006), Zhang et al. (2006), and Yang et al. (2007). One observation on ant colony behavior which has largely been ignored by existing studies is that the ants optimize on two separate variables (shortest distance and safety of route), incorporating multipronged searches and most likely taking into account multiple disturbances to the pheromone trail.

For this study, an experiment was conducted where a single colony of pavement ants Tetramorium caespitum (Linnaeus) was provided with a food source. The path to the food source contained random hazards such as automobiles and human pedestrian traffic. The ants' foraging behavior although random at first was observed very quickly to create a single pheromone trail in a path which was both the closest from a distance standpoint and the safest from an external hazards standpoint. It was hypothesized that the ants optimized on these two variables due to the pheromone trail being disturbed several times. A massive random foraging activity was initially observed where the worker ants went on searching expeditions in all directions for any food sources, resulted in the one path which was most efficient from the perspective of distance and security, i.e., least disturbances to the pheromone trail and shortest distance from the food source. These observations provided additional insights which have been adapted to the ACO program, in this chapter, and are the first of its kind for any ACO programs.

The potential implication of these findings for the ant colony optimization algorithms is improved stability and definitive globally optimal solutions. The improvement in stability stems from the fact that the colony has obtained the least dangerous path, given all the impediments and potential obstacles, to ensure the longevity of survival of the ant colony. Due to the multipronged foraging, in all directions, the ants ensure that the shortest path with the highest security is established, and this is the globally optimal solution for the ants. Consequently, this same principal can be applied to ant colony algorithms by artificially inducing multipronged searches to arrive at the optimal solution, given all the constraints. This globally optimal solution proves to be stable when applied to the population at large. Clustering techniques, such as the *k*-means clustering solution, which is a typical data mining application to which ACO may be applied, could appropriate from the standpoint of the algorithm on a given data set, but may not be very effective when applied to additional data sources. This is due to the algorithm focusing too much on the specific features of an individual data set known as a local optima problem. The multipronged solution-seeking approach of the ant colony solves this problem by growing the colony in search of additional solutions which will enable the algorithm to compare the alternative solutions to the champion solution.

Further observations were conducted in order to obtain any additional insight. Upon observing the ant colony after an efficient and safe path to the food source had been secured, a period of huge growth for the colony was witnessed. The ants steadily increased the size of the column heading to the food source. This phenomenon was attributed to the ants growing the colony up to maximum capacity by having an unlimited food source made available for them to exploit. This growth of the colony ensures the survival of the colony if and when the source of food disappears as there will be more resources to engage in foraging activities. While beyond the scope of this research, these further insights may have some interesting applications to ant hill optimization algorithms and is a scope for further research.

This chapter primarily focuses on applying ant colony optimization as a clustering technique for the financial industry. This chapter is structured as follows. Section 10.2 portrays the advantages of ACO as a means of clustering over *k*-means; Sect. 10.3 describes the methodology adopted in this chapter; and Sect. 10.4 concludes with a summary.

10.2 *k*-Means and Ant Colony Optimization as Clustering Techniques

Clustering aims to discover sensible organization of objects in a given data set by identifying and quantifying similarities (or dissimilarities) between the objects. The central idea is that members within the clusters are alike and members between the clusters are dissimilar. Different criteria can be employed for clustering depending on the application. The ant colony optimization (ACO) is one such clustering method which results in the establishment of the shortest route. In contrast, the *k*-means algorithm is another such criteria used for clustering which attempts to find the centers of natural clusters in the data. *k*-means is a very popular clustering method in the finance industry due to its ability to handle large data sets.

As reported in the existing literature, ant-based clustering has several advantages over the traditional *k*-means technique. For example, ant-based clustering is capable of working with any kind of data that can be described in terms of symmetric dissimilarities, and it imposes no assumption on the shape of the clusters it works with, as against the limiting assumption of *k*-means which presupposes all attributes to be independent and normally distributed. The nature of the ACO algorithm makes it fairly robust to the effects of outliers within the data, whereas the *k*-means algorithm may be sensitive to and does not incorporate any treatment for the outliers. Furthermore, the *k*-means algorithm makes the additional assumption that variance is an appropriate measure of cluster scatter, while the ACO is an autocatalytic method which is based on collective behavior of ants and their pheromone trails, rather than the variance of clusters, and hence results in the establishment of the shortest route. Another attraction of the ACO is that it has a linear scaling behavior, which is suitable for use on large data sets as are frequently encountered today especially in consumer finance, while the *k*-means is preferred for smaller data sets. In general, the ACO performance is more stable and accurate than the *k*-means since in terms of performance, the *k*-means is not guaranteed to return a global optimum. The quality of the final solution depends largely on the initial set of clusters and may, in practice, be much poorer than the global optimum; that is, it can, in fact, converge to the local solution.

In this chapter, a unique method has been set up, to build a hybrid model incorporating the properties of *k*-means clustering algorithm as well as the ant colony algorithm, in order to improve the reliability of the final solution.

10.3 Methodology

This section describes the ant algorithm incorporated in this chapter to solve a typical clustering problem. This chapter closely follows the methodology developed by Shelokar et al. (2003).

10.4 Algorithm Details

The fundamental objective of the algorithm is to obtain the optimal assignment of "N" objects to "K" clusters, based on the "n" attributes.

This section provides a step-by-step description of the algorithm used in this chapter.

A typical ant colony optimization (ACO) works through a pheromone matrix which provides the trail the ants will take based on the highest pheromone concentration. To begin with, a pheromone trail matrix ($N \times K$) which governs the allocation of the *i*th individual to the *k*th cluster is generated, with equal values justifying a random allocation.

Consequently, a normalized pheromone matrix is defined where the normalized probability for each element is calculated based on the formula given in (10.1)

$$P_{ij} = \frac{\tau_{ij}}{\sum_{k=1}^{K} \tau_{ik}}, \quad j = 1, \ldots, K \tag{10.1}$$

where "P_{ij}" is the normalized pheromone probability for element "i" belonging to cluster "j" and "τ_{ij}" is the conditioned element "i" belonging to cluster "j". To note, all row-wise summations of the elements in the normalized matrix amount to 1.

As a unique feature, the ACO algorithm developed in this chapter starts from an initial allocation provided by the *k*-means solution. The objective of the algorithm is to provide a solution which is at least superior to that obtained through a traditional k-means segmentation approach.

In a typical k-means segmentation, cluster center values are computed for the data set by means of the Euclidean distance formula as given in (10.2).

$$J = \sum_{j=1}^{k} \sum_{i=1}^{n} \left\| x_i^{(j)} - c_j \right\| \tag{10.2}$$

where $\left\| x_i^{(j)} - c_j \right\|$, a chosen distance measure between a data point $x_i^{(j)}$ and the cluster center c_j, is an indicator of the distance of the N data points from their respective cluster centers. The optimum cluster string S_K-means is attained by minimizing the distance measure in Eq. 10.2 and is further used to provide the seed for the first iteration.

Based on the number of ants specified by the user, from this existing string S_k-means, a collection of strings are created using a stochastic rule. The stochastic rule constitutes of generating a set of random numbers (with values between 0 and 1) from a uniform distribution equal to the length of the solution string. A threshold value, $0 < q0 < 1$, as defined by the user, is employed to alter the cluster assignment if the random number exceeds the threshold value.

Next, the quality of each of the strings generated is asserted through as objective function given in Eq. 10.3.

$$\text{Min } F(w, m) = \sum_{j=1}^{K} \sum_{i-1}^{N} \sum_{v=1}^{n} w_{ij} \left\| x_{iv} - m_{jv} \right\|^2 \tag{10.3}$$

where x_{iv} is a value of vth attribute of ith sample; m is a cluster center matrix with m_{jv} as an average of the vth attribute of the jth cluster given as follows:

$$m_{jv} = \frac{\sum_{i=1}^{N} w_{ij} x_{iv}}{\sum_{i=1}^{N} w_{ij}}, \quad j = 1, \ldots, K, \quad v = 1, \ldots, n \tag{10.4}$$

The weight matrix is computed using the formula seen in (10.5).

$$\begin{aligned} w_{ij} &= 1, \text{if object } i \text{ is contained in cluster } j \\ w_{ij} &= 0, \text{otherwise} \end{aligned} \tag{10.5}$$

$$i = 1, \ldots, N, \quad j = 1, \ldots, K$$

Further, these strings are sorted by the objective function value in a descending order, from best to worst.

In order to enhance the solution discovered by the ants, a local search procedure is employed on the sorted string obtained in the previous step. Typically, the user defines the extent of the local searches supported by the algorithm, which is set at

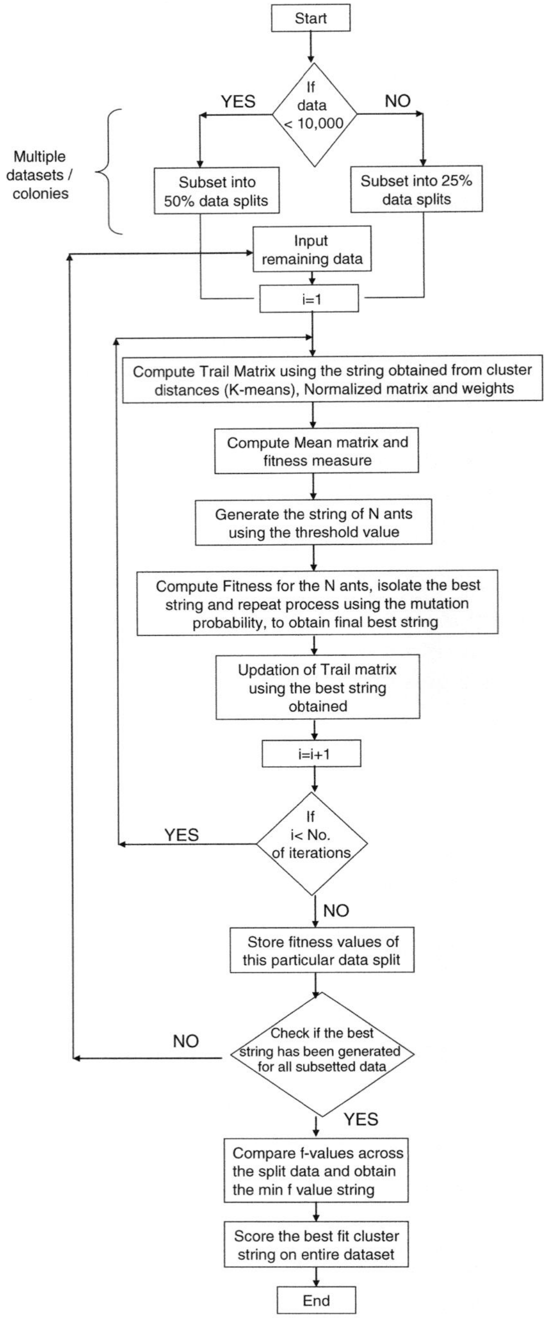

Fig. 10.1 Summary of ant algorithm for data clustering

20 % by default. A genetic algorithm-based mutational approach is employed to conduct the local searches where the mutation threshold is user defined and set to 0.01 in this algorithm. However, local search solutions are retained to the extent they outperform the existing strings.

Once the best string has been identified, the original pheromone matrix is updated using Eq. 10.6.

$$\begin{aligned} &\tau_{ij}(t+1) = (1-\rho)\tau_{ij}(t) + \sum_{l=1}^{L} \Delta\tau_{ij}^{l} \\ &j = 1, \ldots, K, \quad v = 1, \ldots, n \end{aligned} \tag{10.6}$$

where ρ is the persistence of trail that lies between [0, 1] and $(1-\rho)$ the evaporation rate. Higher value of ρ suggests that the information gathered in the past iterations is forgotten faster. The amount $\Delta\tau_{ij}^{l}$ is equal to the reciprocal of the best string fitness value, if cluster j is assigned to ith element of the solution and zero otherwise. Note that the pheromone updating approach reflects a dynamic updation, consistent with adaptive and short horizon memory.

The updation continues until the algorithm converges to a stable solution.

Additionally, in order to avoid converging to a local optimum, a multipronged foraging approach is conducted. A simple strategy of splitting the data set based on a stochastic rule is deployed. The rule consists of splitting the data set into a 50–50 sample split if the total number of observations in the data set are less than or equal to 10,000, or else a 25 % sample split. The ACO algorithm described above is run for each sample separately, and a global solution is obtained by searching over these subsample solutions.

The summary of ant algorithm for data clustering is depicted as a flowchart shown in Fig. 10.1.

10.5 Conclusion

An ant colony optimization algorithm to solve clustering problems has been developed in this chapter. The algorithm has been implemented and tested on several simulated and real data sets using the ACO as developed in this chapter; preliminary computational experience is extremely heartening in terms of the superiority of solution found and the processing time required. The any colony optimization tool has been developed based on the algorithm developed in this chapter. Details of the tool are available in the appendix. A limitation of this study is the generalizability of the results to other data sources as this algorithm was only tested in production on financial services data. Further research is necessary on additional sources of data from other domains.

Another suggestion for further research was the observation during the same experiment that the ants incorporate colony growth behavior which has been observed under the existence of a constant food supply. The growth of the colony when food is plentiful creates a stable environment which insures the survival of both the existing colony and the future gene pool. The stability stems from the fact that more resources are available to keep the colony alive in the event that the single or primary food source is removed. Consequently, this same principal can be applied to ant colony algorithms by artificially growing the colony of ants. While beyond the scope of this research, further insights as to how this behavior can modeled may have some interesting applications to ant hill optimization algorithms and should be explored further.

References

Dorigo M, Maniezzo V, Colomi A (1996) The ant system: optimization by a colony of cooperating agents. IEEE Trans Syst Man Cybern Part B 29(1):29–41

Dorigo M, Di Caro G, Gambardella L, M (1999) Ant algorithms for discrete optimization. Artif Life 5(2):137–172

Peters K, Johansson A, Dussutour A, Helbing D (2006) Analytical and numerical investigation of ant behavior under crowded conditions. Adv Comput Syst 9(4):337–352

Shelokar PS, Jayaraman VK, Kulkarni BD (2003) An ant colony approach for clustering. Anal Chim Acta 59:187–195

Yang Z, Yu B, Chang C (2007) A parallel ant colony algorithm for bus network optimization. Comput Aided Civ Infrastruct Eng 22:44–55

Zhang J, Hu X, Tan X, Zhong JH, Huang Q (2006) Implementation of an ant colony optimization technique for job shop scheduling problem. Trans Inst Meas Control 28(1):93–108

Chapter 11
Customer Lifecycle Value—Past, Present, and Future

Avanti George, Saumitra N. Bhaduri and David Fogarty

Abstract In the modern environment of service-based marketing techniques, maximizing customer lifetime value has evolved into a crucial objective of CRM, in order to obtain profits from creating and sustaining long-term relationships with their customers. This chapter makes a contribution by reviewing the various CLV techniques and modeling advances in this area and in addition highlights the direction for development. It specifically addresses the key challenges in the literature with regard to integrating dynamic, macroeconomic aspects into the CLV which has become imminent given the current economic and financial turmoil.

11.1 Introduction

In recent years, significant activities, in both managerial practices and academia, have emerged around the concept of customer relationship management (CRM). Successful customer management begins with acquiring the right customers. Customer acquisition has been very much an empirical question and not much been addressed in academic research. Most businesses indiscriminately apply a hunting mentality and seem to believe that every new customer is a good customer. Although this indiscriminate acquisition approach might contain some truth, especially in growing markets, in highly mature and saturated markets, it clearly is suboptimal. Businesses have found that more customers are not necessarily better, but more of the right customers are (Reinartz et al. 2005).

The most generic form of an acquisition process involves three specific steps. First, the decision maker selects an objective function to pursue, e.g., maximum response possibility or maximum revenue. The next step involves profiling existing customers as attractive according to the previously chosen objective function. Third, the ideal customer profile based on his/her maximum economic value gets extracted and generated for all persons in the prospect pool. This maximization of

This chapter contains contributions from Avanti George, Madras School of Economics, Chennai, India.

S.N. Bhaduri and D. Fogarty, *Advanced Business Analytics*,
DOI 10.1007/978-981-10-0727-9_11

the economic customer value for the business is the key objective in CRM principles.

The heart of CRM activities is differential, systematic resource allocations to customers with different economic values for the organization. As mentioned above, fundamental to this is the notion of customer's economic value to a business. Businesses attempt to maximize the customer's economic value, thereby linking the concept of economic value to the metric of customer lifecycle value (CLV), i.e., the net present value of discounted cash-flows over time.

Customer lifecycle value (CLV) is gaining increasing significance as marketing metric. There are several factors that account for the growing interest in this concept. First, there is an ever-increasing pressure to make marketing accountable and conventional marketing metrics such as sales, fall short of showing returns on marketing investment. Second, although financial metrics such as stock price and aggregate profit of the business unit are useful measures, they have narrow analytical capability. Studies have found that not all customers are equally profitable and such aggregate financial measures therefore do not allow for differential diagnostics. In contrast, CLV is a disaggregate metric that can be used to identify profitable customers and allocate resources accordingly (Kumar and Reinartz 2006). Third, advances in information technology have resulted in enormous amount of customer transaction data, which allows for firms to use data on revealed preferences rather than intentions. Furthermore, sampling is no longer necessary when the entire customer base is available. Current technology makes it possible to leverage insights from the data and customize marketing programs for individual customers.

In spite of the high level of sophistication of the CLV calculations, there still exists a gap in the literature with regard to integrating dynamic, macroeconomy aspects into the CLV. Relatively, there is little empirical research to understand how the underlying economy affects customers' subsequent financial product purchase behaviors. A better understanding of this influence and being able to predict the probability of purchasing are important for financial services industries. The current literature is restricted to a semidynamic, time-invariant methodology. Because of the challenges associated with forecasting future revenue streams, most empirical research on "lifecycle value" computes customer profitability based solely on customers' past behavior. But in order to be true to the notion of CLV, the measures should look to the future, not the past. In light of the current worldwide recession, there are several highly volatile factors that need to be taken into account, which would potentially have a large impact on the CLV. In this environment, the question of the ability to use past data to predict the future gains further importance. Rules need to be created to guide the marketing manager to undertake actions that maximize the value of the portfolio, in situations of an unstable economy.

The purpose of this chapter is to describe the existing academic models and approaches that are used to obtain the CLV for CRM applications in the existing literature. It takes stock of the various nuances in CLV modeling and proposes an integrated framework to incorporate time variant exogenous factors that result in a dynamic CLV function. The chapter is organized as follows. Section 11.2 portrays a simplified version of the CLV. Section 11.3 depicts the two basic categories of CLV calculation, i.e., the probability based models and the econometric models. Section 11.4 discusses possible extensions to the current literature beyond the static nature of CLV calculations. The extensions of the current literature shift the realm of CLV into a more realistic dynamic approach that incorporates future economic forecasts as a key driver in its calculations. Finally, Sect. 11.5 concludes the chapter.

11.2 Fundamentals of CLV

The metric CLV is the present value of all future profits obtained from a customer over his or her life of relationship with a firm. CLV is computed via the discounted cash flow approach used in finance. However, there are two key differences. First, CLV is typically defined and estimated at an individual customer or segment level. This allows us to identify those customers who are more profitable than others rather than simply examining average profitability. Further, unlike finance, CLV explicitly incorporates the possibility that a customer may defect to competitors in the future.

A simplified form of CLV for a customer can be represented as follows:

$$\mathrm{CLV} = \sum_{t=0}^{T} \frac{(p_t - c_t)r_t}{(1+i)^t} - \mathrm{AC}$$

where

p_t price paid by a consumer at time t,
c_t direct cost of servicing the customer at time t,
i discount rate or cost of capital for the firm,
r_t probability of customer repeat buying or being "alive" at time t,
AC acquisition cost,
T time horizon for estimating CLV

Despite this straightforward formulation, researchers have used different variations in modeling and estimating CLV. Some have used an arbitrary time horizon or expected customer lifetime (Reinartz and Kumar 2000; Thomas 2001), whereas others have used an infinite time horizon (e.g., Fader et al. 2005; Gupta et al. 2004). Gupta and Lehmann (2005) showed that using an expected customer lifetime generally overestimates CLV, sometimes quite substantially.

It is also important to point out that some modeling approaches ignore competition because of the lack of competitive data. Finally, how frequently the CLV is updated depends on the dynamics of a particular market. For example, in markets where margins and retention may change dramatically over a short period of time (e.g., due to competitive activity), it may be appropriate to re-estimate CLV more frequently. Researchers either build separate models for customer acquisition, retention, and margin or sometimes combine these components. For example, Thomas (2001), Reinartz et al. (2005) simultaneously captured customer acquisition and retention. Fader et al. (2005) captured recency and frequency in one model and built a separate model for monetary value. However, the approaches for modeling these components or CLV differ across researchers.

In the following section, two specific CLV modeling approaches, typically used by researchers, will be discussed in detail.

11.3 CLV Approaches in Literature

11.3.1 Probability Based Models

A probability model is an illustration of the world in which observed behavior is governed by unobserved behavioral characteristics, which in turn may vary across individuals. The focus of the model-building effort is on telling a simple story that describes the observed behavior instead of trying to explain differences in observed behavior as a function of covariates (as is the case with any regression model). The modeler typically assumes that consumers' behavior varies across the population according to some probability distribution.

For the purposes of computing CLV, predictions need to be made, about whether an individual will still be an active customer in the future and, if so, what his or her purchasing behavior. One of the first models to explicitly address these issues is the Pareto/NBD model developed by Schmittlein et al. (1987) which describes the flow of transactions in non-contractual setting. It requires only two pieces of information about each customer's past purchasing history: his "recency" (when his last transaction occurred) and "frequency" (how many transactions he made in a specified time period). Using these two key summary statistics, Schmittlein et al. derive expressions for a number of managerially relevant quantities, such as the probability that an individual is still active given his observed purchasing behavior, and the expected number of transactions in the next period (e.g., year) conditional on the customer's observed purchasing behavior.

Within the direct marketing literature, there is a strong tradition of classifying customers on the basis of their "RFM" characteristics. Given the basic recognition that future behavior is correlated with past behavior, this has proven to be a fruitful paradigm for many researchers and practitioners.

However, in recent times there has been a significant shift from traditional RFM-based CLV models to the iso-value approach introduced by Fader et al. (2004). Under the iso-value approach customers with equivalent future value despite differences in their past behavior are depicted through iso-value plots as seen in Fig. 11.1. The iso-value curve clearly brings out how higher recency and higher frequency are correlated with greater future purchasing and higher values of CLV. The shape of these curves is fairly intuitive. Therefore, the creation and analysis of iso-value curves is an excellent way to summarize and evaluate the CLV for an entire customer base. It can help guide managerial decision making and

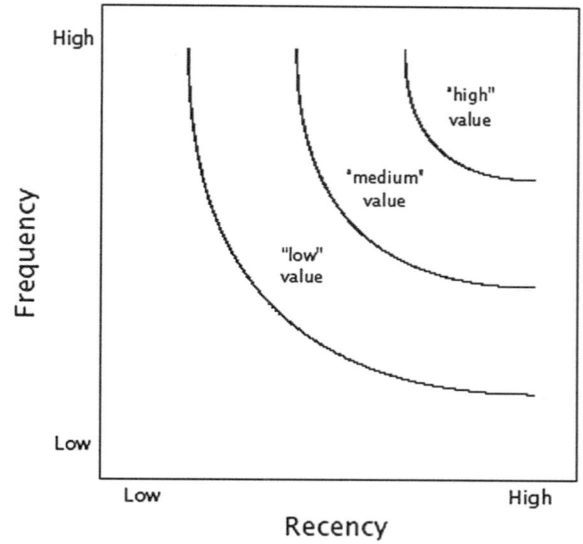

Fig. 11.1 Relationship between recency/frequency and CLV

provide accurate quantitative benchmarks to better gauge the "return on investment" for programs that companies use to develop and manage their portfolio of customers.

Further, the iso-value approach has several distinctive advantages over the traditional RFM approach[1]: First, the standard RFM-based approach tends to omit sources of heterogeneity other than recency, frequency, and monetary value and does not take advantage of the customer's longitudinal purchase history. Second, the iso-value approach (Fader et al. 2004) using well-established stochastic models of buying behavior (Schmittlein et al. 1987) makes not only a next period prediction but also forecasts for periods beyond that. Assuming that monetary value is independent of the underlying transaction process, Fader et al. (2004) show that the future value of customers can be represented by information on recency and frequency alone. The iso-value approach does a better job uncovering the interactions among input parameters than traditional regression. For example, for customers who made a relatively large number of transactions in the past, recency plays a disproportionate role in determining their CLV. In addition, the iso-value model can capture the "increasing frequency" paradox as depicted in Fig. 11.2.

[1]The RFM model is a good benchmark when considering non-contractual settings where transaction can occur at any point in time. It is not an appropriate model for any contractual business settings. Nor is it an appropriate model for non-contractual settings where transactions can only occur at fixed (discrete) points in time, such as attendance at annual conferences, arts festivals, as in such settings, the assumption of Poisson purchasing is not relevant. Thus, models such as Fader et al. (2004) iso-value, beta-binominal/beta-geometric (BG/BB) model, or Morrison et al.'s (1982) brand loyal with exit model would be appropriate alternatives.

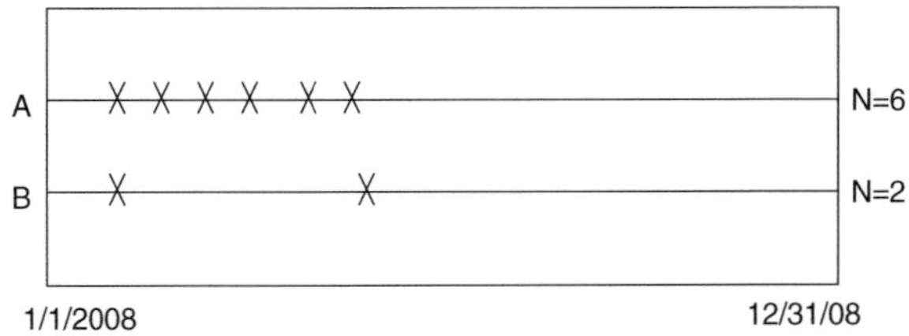

Fig. 11.2 Iso-value model

If it is assumed that customers A and B were active on Dec 31, 2008, it is expected that customer A to have a greater CLV given his/her higher number of prior transactions, but the pattern strongly suggests customer A is no longer active. Conversely, customer B has a lower underlying purchase rate, so the future CLV of customer B is much higher on Dec 1 than is that of customer A. While a regression-based scoring model would miss this pattern and lead to faulty inferences, the iso-value approach captures these effects properly.

Iso-Value Approach:

Fader et al. (2004) as a part of their iso-value approach derived the explicit formula for the expected lifetime revenue stream associated with a customer with "recency," "frequency" (in a time period of length T), and an average transaction value of m_x, with continuous compounding at rate of interest. The following section provides a brief description of the iso-value approach by Fader et al. (2005).

They propose the CLV as a product of the number of discounted expected transactions (DET) and a value "multiplier" to yield an overall estimate of lifecycle value:

$$\text{CLV} = \text{margin} * \text{revenue}/\text{transaction} * \text{DET} \tag{11.1}$$

Closely, following Schmittlein et al.'s (1987) model, Fader et al. (2004) proposed to estimate the DET under the ensuing assumptions: First, a customer's relationship with the firm has two phases: in the first phase, the customer is "alive" for an indefinite period of time, and, then subsequently moves into the second phase by becoming permanently inactive. Second, while "alive," the number of transactions made by a customer can be characterized by a Poisson process. Third, each customer's unobserved "life cycle" is distributed exponential. Fourth, heterogeneity in dropout rates across customers follows a gamma distribution. And finally, the transaction rates and the dropout rates vary independently across customers.[2]

A customer's purchase transaction can be represented in binary terms as 1 for purchase and 0 for no purchase. A transaction stream is represented as (x, n, m) where x is the number of purchases occurred in n transaction opportunities with the last transaction happening at $m \leq n$. For example, reading from left to right, the purchase string 0 1 0 1 1 0 0 0 can be summarized as (x = 3, n = 8, m = 5). Given

[2]The second and third assumptions result in the NBD, whereas the next two assumptions yield the Pareto distribution. This model requires only two pieces of information about each customer's past purchasing history: his or her "recency" (when his or her last transaction occurred) and "frequency" (how many transactions he or she made in a specified time period).

this summary of purchase transaction behavior, the model tries to estimate the probability of activeness and expected number of transaction in a specific future time period. More generally for a customer with a purchase transaction history (x, t_x, T), where x is the number of transactions observed in the time period (0, T]; and t_x ($0 < t_x \leq T$) is the time of the last transaction; is used to estimate a number of relevant quantities, including:

$E[X(t)]$, the expected number of transactions in a time period of length t, which is central to computing the expected transaction volume for the whole customer base over time; $P(\text{alive})|X = x, t_x, T)$, the probability that an individual with observed behavior (x, t_x, T) is still an active customer at time T; and $E(Y(t)|X = x, t_x, T)$, the expected number of transactions in the period $(T, T + t)$ for an individual with observed behavior (x, t_x, T). Details of the derivation are available in Bhaduri et al.

Fader et al. (2004) compute the present value of the expected future transaction stream for a customer with purchase history $(X = x, t_x, T)$, with continuous compounding at rate of interest δ, for a Pareto/NBD model as follows:

$$\begin{aligned} &\text{DET}(\delta|r, \alpha, s, \beta, X = x, t_x, T) \\ &= \frac{\alpha^r \beta^s \delta^{s-1} \tau(r+x+1)\varphi(s,s;\delta(\beta+T))}{\tau(r)(\alpha+T)^{r+x+1} L(r,\alpha,s,\beta|X=x,t_x,T)} \end{aligned} \qquad (11.2)$$

where r, α, s, β are the Pareto/NBD parameters; $\varphi(\cdot)$ is the confluent hyper-geometric function of the second kind; and $L(\cdot)$ is the Pareto/NBD likelihood function. The derivation of this expression for DET is central to our CLV estimation.

As required in the CLV calculations represented in Eq. (11.1), the second step in the iso-value approach involves building a separate model for dollar expenditure per transaction.

A general model of monetary value is specified keeping the following three assumptions in mind.[3] First, the dollar value of a customer's given transaction varies randomly around his average transaction value. Second, average transaction values vary across customers but do not vary over time for any given individual. Third, the distribution of average transaction values across customers is independent of the transaction process.

In order to arrive at an expression for our desired quantity, $E(M|m_x, x)$, the Bayes' theorem is employed to derive the posterior distribution of ν for a customer with an average spend of m_x across x transactions:

[3]Various attempts have been made in the past to model CLV including Schmittlein and Peterson (1994) where they assume that the random purchasing around the individual's mean is characterized by a normal distribution and that the average transactions values are distributed across the population according to a normal distribution. This implies that the overall distribution of transaction values can be characterized by a normal distribution. Fader (2004) adopts the gamma–gamma model originally proposed by Colombo and Jiang (1999).

$$g(v|p,q,\gamma,m_x,x) = \frac{(\gamma+m_x x)^{px+q} v^{px+q-1} e^{-v(\gamma+m_x x)}}{\tau(px+q)} \quad (11.3)$$

which is itself a gamma distribution with shape parameter $px+q$ and scale parameter γ + m_x x. It follows that the expected average transaction value for a customer with an average spend of m_x across x transactions is,

$$E(M|p,q,\gamma,m_x,x) = \frac{(\gamma+m_x x)p}{px+q-1} = \left(\frac{(q-1)}{(px+q-1)}\right)\frac{\gamma p}{q-1} + \left(\frac{px}{px+q-1}\right)m_x \quad (11.4)$$

This is a weighted average of the population mean, $\gamma p/(q-1)$ and the observed average transaction value, m_x. It should be clear that larger values of x will see less weight being placed on the population mean and more weight on the observed customer-level average of m_x. However, one of the limiting assumptions is that recency/frequency and monetary value are independent. This assumption has been relaxed in Glady et al. (2007) to obtain a modified Pareto/NBD, with the interaction effects between the dollar values of transactions with the frequency of transactions. They have demonstrated that the dependence between the number of transactions and their profitability can be used to increase the accuracy of the prediction of CLV, by estimating them jointly.

In the next section, an alternative approach to CLV through the econometric models is discussed. Though many econometric models share the underlying philosophy of the probability models, it is worth reviewing some of the significant techniques in this area.[4]

11.4 Econometric Models

Most of the econometric studies address customer acquisition, retention, default, and expansion (cross-selling or margin) in order to combine them to estimate customer lifecycle value or CLV. A simplified version of the CLV can be represented as follows:

$$\text{CLV} = R - C - L \quad (11.5)$$

The three components of the CLV are lifecycle revenue (*R*), acquisition cost (*C*), and loss (*L*), discounted at an appropriate rate. The revenue component relies on income earned through cross-sell and up-sell, while the cost component is based on

[4]Specifically, studies that use hazard models to estimate customer retention are similar to the NBD/Pareto models except for the fact that the former may use more general hazard functions and typically incorporate covariates.

the net debt on books. The loss component consists of loss due to delinquency and charge-offs.

A typical framework can be represented as follows:

$$\begin{aligned} \mathrm{CLV} = \lambda\{ & [P_{\mathrm{ET}}(Rev_{\mathrm{ET}}) + (1 - P_{\mathrm{ET}})(Rev_{\mathrm{FT}})] \\ & + P_{xs}(Rev_{X-\mathrm{sell}}) + P_{\mathrm{up}}(Rev_{\mathrm{up-sell}}) \\ & - (\mathrm{CF}) - l * B@R\} \end{aligned} \tag{11.6}$$

where Rev_{ET} is the revenue earned from the early terminated accounts; Rev_{FT} is the revenue earned from full term customers; $Rev_{X-\mathrm{sell}}$ is the revenue earned through cross-selling; $Rev_{\mathrm{up-sell}}$ is the revenue earned through an up-sell; P_{xs} is the likelihood of a cross-sell; P_{up} is the likelihood of an up-sell; and CF is the cost of funds. λ is the probability of response and $l * B@R$ is the product of the probability of default and the balance at risk (loss component). All numbers are discounted at an appropriate rate.

In the following section, each of the dimensions of the CLV and its current state of development are addressed.

11.4.1 Customer Acquisition

Customer acquisition refers to the first-time purchase by new or lapsed customers. Research in this area focuses on the factors that influence buying decisions of these new customers. It also attempts to link acquisition with customers' retention behavior as well as CLV. The basic model for customer acquisition is a logit or a probit (Gensch 1984; Thomas 2001; Thomas et al. 2004). Specifically, customer j at time t (i.e., Y_{jt} = 1) is modeled as follows:

$$\begin{aligned} Y_{jt}^* &= \alpha_j X_{jt} + \varepsilon_{jt} \\ Y_{jt} &= 1 \quad \text{if } Y_{jt}^* > 0 \\ Y_{jt} &= 0 \quad \text{if } Y_{jt}^* \leq 0 \end{aligned} \tag{11.7}$$

where X_{jt} are the covariates and α_j are consumer-specific response parameters. Depending on the assumption of the error term, one can obtain a logit or a probit model (Lewis 2005b; Thomas 2001).

In contrast to the early work (Blattberg and Deighton 1996) assuming acquisition and retention to be independent, more recent work (Hansotia and Wang 1997) in this area have indirectly linked, these two outcomes by using a logit model for acquisition and a right-censored Tobit model for CLV. More recently, several authors have explicitly linked acquisition and retention (Thomas 2001; Thomas et al. 2004). Using data for airline pilots' membership, Thomas (2001) showed the importance of linking acquisition and retention decisions. She found that ignoring this link can lead to CLV estimates that are 6–52 % different from her model.[5] The dynamics of pricing was also examined by Lewis (2005a) using a dynamic programming approach. He found that for new customers, price sensitivity increases with time lapsed, whereas for current customers, it decreases with time.

11.4.2 Customer Retention/Activity

Customer retention is the probability of a customer being "alive" or buying repeatedly from a firm. In contractual settings, customers inform the firm when they terminate their relationship. However, in non-contractual settings (e.g., financial services), a firm has to infer whether a customer is still active. Most companies define a customer as active based on simple rules of thumb.[6] In contrast, researchers rely on statistical models to assess the probability of retention. However, it is important to note that the research on retention not only attracted a number of techniques but also prompted numerous studies with trends of divergent conclusions.[7] There are two broad classes of retention models. The first class of model

[5]Thomas et al. (2004a) found that whereas low price increased the probability of acquisition, it reduced the relationship duration. Therefore, customers who may be inclined to restart a relationship may not be the best customers in terms of retention. Thomas et al. (2004) empirically validated this across two industries. They also found that customers should be acquired based on their profitability rather than on the basis of the cost to acquire and retain them. Lewis (2003) showed how promotions that enhance customer acquisition may be detrimental in the long run. He found that if new customers for a new chapter subscription were offered regular price, their renewal probability was 70 %. However, this dropped to 35 % for customers who were acquired through a $1 weekly discount. Similar effects were found in the context of Internet grocery where renewal probabilities declined from 40 % for regular-priced acquisitions to 25 % for customers acquired through a $10 discount. On average, a 35 % acquisition discount resulted in customers with about half the CLV of regularly acquired customers. In other words, unless these acquisition discounts double the baseline acquisition rate of customers, they would be detrimental to the CE of a firm. These results are consistent with the long-term promotion effects found in the scanner data (Jedidi et al. 1999). In contrast, Anderson and Simester (2004) conducted three field studies and found that deep price discounts have a positive impact on the long-run profitability of first-time buyers but negative long-term impact on established customers.

[6]For example, eBay defines a customer to be active if she or he has bid, bought, or listed on its site during the past 12 months.

[7]The interest in customer retention and customer loyalty increased significantly with the work of Reichheld and Sasser (1990), who found that a 5 % increase in customer retention could increase firm profitability from 25 to 85 %. Reichheld (1996) also emphasized the importance of customer retention. However, Reinartz and Kumar (2000) argued against this result and suggested that "it is the revenue that drives the lifetime value of a customer and not the duration of a customer's tenure" (p. 32). Reinartz and Kumar (2002) further contradicted Reichheld based on their research findings of weak to moderate correlation (0.2–45) between customer tenure and profitability across four data sets. However, a low correlation can occur if the relationship between loyalty and profitability is nonlinear (Bowman and Narayandas 2004).

considers customer defection as permanent or "lost for good" and typically uses hazard models to predict probability of customer defection. The second class considers customer switching to competitors as transient or "always a share." Each class of models is briefly discussed.

11.4.2.1 "Lost for Good"—Hazard-Based Models

Hazard-based models typically fall into two broad groups—accelerated failure time (AFT) and proportional hazard (PH) models.[8]

Kalbfleisch and Prentice (1980) have depicted AFT models in the following form:

$$\text{Ln}(t_j) = \beta_j X_j + \sigma \mu_j \tag{11.8}$$

where t is the purchase duration for customer j and X are the covariates. If $\sigma = 1$ and μ has an extreme value distribution, then an exponential duration model with constant hazard rate is obtained. Different specifications of σ and μ lead to different models such as Weibull or generalized gamma, e.g., Allenby et al. (1999), Lewis (2003), Venkatesan and Kumar (2004) used a generalized gamma for modeling relationship duration.

In contrast, Proportional hazard-based duration specify the hazard rate (λ) as a function of baseline hazard rate (λ_o) and covariates

$$\lambda(t, X) = \lambda_o(t) \exp(\beta X) \tag{11.9}$$

This approach was used by Bolton (1998), Gonul et al. (2000), Knott et al. (2002), Levinthal and Fichman (1988). Different specifications for the baseline hazard rate provide different duration models such as exponential, Weibull, or Gompertz.

Yet another alternative focuses on customer retention or churn as a binary outcome leading to a form of discrete-time hazard model. Typically, the model takes the form of a logit or probit. Due to its simplicity and ease of estimation, this approach is commonly used in the industry.

In earlier chapter, a new class of models is discussed to predict attrition, called the double hurdle model. In these models, two dynamic elements are simultaneously addressed: Whether or not a customer would attrite and, if yes, then when will he attrite in the course of his life cycle. A consumer in a double hurdle framework must cross two hurdles in order to attrite. The "first hurdle" needs to be crossed in

---

[8]In survival analysis, an AFT model is a parametric model that provides an alternative to the commonly used PH models. Whereas a PH model assumes that the effect of a covariate is to multiply the hazard by some constant, an AFT model assumes that the effect of a covariate is to multiply the predicted event time by some constant. In both, the AFT parametric and the PH parametric approaches, the Weibull distribution is the most commonly used.

order to be a potential attritor. Given that the borrower is a potential attritor, their current circumstances then dictate whether or not they do in fact attrite—the "second hurdle."

The double hurdle model contains two equations.

$$d_i^* = z_i'\alpha + \varepsilon_i$$

$$y_i^{**} = x_i'\beta + u_i$$

$$\begin{pmatrix} \varepsilon_i \\ u_i \end{pmatrix} \sim N\left[\begin{pmatrix} 0 \\ 0 \end{pmatrix}, \begin{pmatrix} 1 & 0 \\ 0 & \sigma^2 \end{pmatrix}\right] \tag{11.10}$$

The first hurdle is then represented by the following:

$$\begin{aligned} d_i &= 1 \text{ if } d_i^* \geq 0 \\ d_i &= 0 \text{ if } d_i^* \leq 0 \end{aligned} \tag{11.11}$$

While, the first hurdle (in Eq. 11.11) is close to a probit representation, the second hurdle (in Eq. 11.13) closely resembles the Tobit model.

The log-likelihood function for the double hurdle is

$$\begin{aligned} \text{Log}\, L &= \sum_0 \text{In}\left[1 - \Phi(z_i'\alpha)\Phi\left(\frac{x_i'\beta}{\sigma}\right)\right] \\ &+ \sum_+ \text{In}\left[\Phi(z_i'\alpha)\frac{1}{\sigma}\phi\left(\frac{y_i - x_i'\beta}{\sigma}\right)\right] \end{aligned} \tag{11.12}$$

$$y_i^* = \max\left(y_i^{**}, 0\right) \tag{11.13}$$

Finally, the observed variable y_i is determined as follows:

$$\text{Expected Lifetime} = d_i y_i^*$$

11.4.2.2 "Always a Share"—Markov Models

In the second class of models, customers are allowed to switch among competitors and this is generally modeled using a Markov model. These models estimate transition probabilities of a customer being in a certain state. Pfeifer and Carraway (2000) defined them based on customers' recency of purchases as well as an additional state for new or former customers. Rust, Lemon, and Zeithaml (2004) defined the transition probability as brand switching probabilities that vary over time as per a logit model.[9]

[9]Rust et al. (2004) argued that the "lost for good" approach understates CLV because it does not allow a defected customer to return. Others have argued that this is not a serious problem because customers can be treated as renewable resource (Dréze and Bonfrer 2005) and lapsed customers

11.4.3 Customer Margin and Expansion

The third component of CLV is the margin generated by a customer in each time period t. This margin depends on a customer's past purchase behavior as well as a firm's efforts in cross-selling and up-selling products to the customer. There are two broad approaches used in the literature to capture margin. One set of studies model margin directly while the other set of studies explicitly model cross-selling. Both approaches are briefly discussed.

Several authors have made the assumption that margins for a customer remain constant over the future time horizon. Reinartz and Kumar (2006) used average contribution margin of a customer based on his or her prior purchase behavior to project CLV. Gupta et al. (2004) also used constant margin based on history. Gupta and Lehmann (2005) showed that in many industries this may be a reasonable assumption. Venkatesan and Kumar (2004) used a simple regression model to capture changes in contribution margin over time. Specifically, they suggested that change in contribution margin for customer j at time t is given as follows:

$$\Delta \text{CM}_{jt} = \beta X_{jt} + e_{jr} \quad (11.14)$$

The second group of studies has explicitly modeled cross-selling, which in turn improves customer margin over time. One of the keys to success in consumer financial services is the ability to convert the short-term customer relationships into long-term relationships through effective CRM. This can be achieved through cross-sell and up-sell of products to the customers. With the rising cost of customer acquisition, firms are increasingly interested in cross-selling more products and services to their existing customers. However, an effective cross-sell and up-sell strategy requires a good understanding of different classes of customers and the possible opportunities to market different products, line extensions, and new product categories. It is also important to understand the customers' propensity to respond to various offers and, the best time to make the right offers. This requires a better understanding of which products to cross-sell, to whom, and at what time. In many product categories, such as books, music, entertainment, and sports, it is common for firms to use recommendation systems. A good example of this is the recommendation system used by Amazon. Earlier recommendation systems were built on the concept of collaborative filtering. Recently, some researchers have used Bayesian approach for creating more powerful recommendation systems (Ansari et al. 2000).

(Footnote 9 continued)

can be reacquired (Thomas et al. 2004). It is possible that the choice of the modeling approach depends on the context. For example, in many industries (e.g., cellular phone, cable, and banks), customers are usually monogamous and maintain their relationship with only one company. In other contexts (e.g., consumer goods, airlines, and business-to-business relationship), consumers simultaneously conduct business with multiple companies, and the "always a share" approach may be more suitable.

In some other product categories, such as financial services, customers acquire products in a natural sequence. For example, a customer may start her or his relationship with a bank with a checking and/or savings account and over time buy more complex products such as mortgage and brokerage service. Kamakura et al. (1991) argued that customers are likely to buy products when they reach a "financial maturity" commensurate with the complexity of the product. Recently, Li et al. (2005) used a similar conceptualization for cross-selling sequentially ordered financial products.

Verhoef et al. (2001) used an ordered probit to model consumers' cross-buying. Knott et al. (2002) used logit, discriminant analysis, and neural networks models to predict the next product to buy and found that all models performed roughly the same and significantly better (predictive accuracy of 40–45 %) than random guessing (accuracy of 11–15 %). Finally, Kumar et al. (2006) showed that cross-selling efforts produced a significant increase in profits per customer when using a model that accounts for dependence in choice and timing of purchases.

11.5 The Future of CLV

In today's context, with the recent credit crisis deepening, the vital question to be addressed is the reliability of the use of past data to predict the future. Despite the high level of sophistication of the CLV calculations, there still exists a gap in the literature with regard to integrating the dynamic, macroeconomy aspects into the CLV. Based on the state of the modeling tools as reflected in the current academic literature and the needs of the cutting-edge industry practitioners, the following methods have been identified, that represent opportunities for tackling the issue at hand.

11.5.1 Moving Beyond Static Hazard Models

One of the extensions to the conventional CLV approaches this chapter proposes is similar to Tang et al. (2005), which incorporates the impact of socio-demographic and economic variables on the probability of purchasing financial products.

The proportional hazard model version of the Weibull model is considered where

$$h^s(t) = e^{k(\alpha.x + \beta\cdot y(s+t))} h_0(t) \tag{11.15}$$

The chapter proposes a dynamic base line hazard function $h_0(t)$ which not only incorporate X, vector of static socio-demographic characteristics of the customer, but also and $y(s)$, the vector of external economic condition variables at time s. The objective of the specification is that it can track the interaction between the socio-demographic and economic variables, thereby improving the accuracy of the forecast of future purchase.

11.5.2 Reconciling Future Uncertainties Using Fuzzy Logic

One of the drivers of the growing interest in CLV in recent times has been the firm's ability to collect a large amount of historical data. A number of models have been developed that can provide insights of future behavior, using such data. However, one recognizes the inherent limitation of developing a CLV model based on precise transaction data where the factors underlying the customer lifecycle value are dynamic in nature and cannot be captured with precision. Therefore, to obtain richer insights it may be worthwhile to augment the historical data through a series of qualitative information on competitive behavior, economic conditions, and attitudinal behavior. This chapter proposes a Fuzzy logic framework to integrate the qualitative information with the historical data.

Fuzzy logic has numerous advantages over the traditional statistical methods. The performance of a fuzzy expert system is not dependent on the volume of historical data available. It can handle uncertain, input variable values, like forecasts and it deals with vague and inexact input variables values such as the state of the economy. Also, since these systems produce a result based on logical linguistic rules, extreme data points in a small data set do not unduly influence these models. Most importantly, in the context of extending the CLV to incorporate uncertainties of the macroeconomy, the use of dynamic and adaptable fuzzy models enables the inclusion of different values at different time periods as input variables and finds flexible solutions to such dynamic changes by utilizing fuzzy sets instead of exact values.

11.5.3 Recognizing the Need to Model Rare Events

Within the field of marketing, models that are developed are typically applied to situations where the event occurs with some frequency, such as customer attrition or customer response. However, when these models are applied to a situation where the predicted behavior is extremely rare, there is a high possibility for them to breakdown. For example, when modeling macroeconomic business events, such as stock market bubbles or crashes, and recessions, purely categorical forecasts using the logit model is inherently risky. Therefore, there are gains to be sought from the insights obtained from the statistics literature on the modeling of rare events. The alphabet model provides a formalism for understanding the role of rare events.

11.5.4 Scope of Bayesian Framework to Overcome Future Uncertainties

As mentioned earlier, quantitative analysis in marketing, hinge on models which are used for forecasting and planning and therefore frequently require sizeable historical data, to obtain the future forecasts. However, there are built-in constraints from relying on precise transaction data, to develop the CLV model where the factors underlying the customer lifecycle value are dynamic in nature and cannot be captured accurately. Bayesian methods can be effectively used to obtain early forecasts without relying heavily on the historical data. The Bayesian techniques, model parameters from previously existing cases or from smaller data, and these initial parameter estimates can be updated as and when the data becomes available. Bayesian models use prior beliefs and transform it into a statistic so that inferences can be made about the customers. The prior distribution also allows the ability to incorporate the knowledge or experience of the manager by augmenting a likely range of values of the parameters into the analysis. As data become available for the product, this prior distribution is updated by Bayes theorem, and the forecasts adapt to the unique features of the product.

11.6 Conclusion

As marketing aims to become more accountable, CLV has emerged as one of the new metrics that help assess the return on marketing investment. The easy availability of transaction data and increasing sophistication in modeling has made CLV an increasingly important concept in both academia and practice.

This chapter makes a contribution by reviewing the various CLV techniques and modeling advances in this area and also highlights the direction for development. It specifically addresses the key challenges of gaps in the literature with regard to integrating dynamic, macroeconomy aspects into the CLV. It identifies scope for enhancement of the CLV given the current economic situation. Further expansion of the principal illustrated here will auger powerful business possibilities and should be a fruitful area of research.

References

Allenby G, Robert L, Lichung J (1999) A dynamic model of purchase timing with application to direct marketing. J Am Stat Assoc 94:365–74

Ansari A, Skander E, Rajeev K (2000) Internet recommendation systems. J Mark Res 40:131–45

Blattberg R, John D (1996) Managing marketing by the customer equity test. Harvard Business Review 75 (4):136–44

Bolton, Ruth N (1998) A dynamic model of the duration of the customer's relationship with a continuous service provider: The role of satisfaction. Market Sci 17 (1):46–65
Fader PS, Bruce GSH, Paul DB (2004) Customer-base analysis with discrete-time transaction data. Unpublished working paper
Fader PS, Bruce GSH, Lee KL (2005) RFM and CLV: using Iso-CLV curves for customer base analysis. J Market Res 42:415–30
Gensch, Dennis H (1984) Targeting the switchable industrial customer. J Market Sci 3 (1):41–54
Gonul F, Kim B-D, Shi M (2000) Mailing smarter to catalog customers. J Interact Market 14 (2):2–16
Gupta S, Lehmann DR (2003) Customers as assets. J Interact Market 17(1):9–24
Gupta S, Lehmann DR, Jennifer AS (2004) Valuing customers. J Market Res 41 (1):7–18
Gupta S, Lehmann DR (2005) Managing customers as investments. Wharton School Publishing, Philadelphia
Hansotia B, Paul W (1997) Analytical challenges in customer acquisition. J Dir Market 11 (2):7–19
Kalbfleisch J, Ross P (1980) Statistical analysis of failure time data. Wiley, New York
Kamakura W, Sridhar R, Rajendra S (1991) Applying latent trait analysis in the evaluation of prospects for cross-selling of financial services. Int J Res Market 8:329–349
Knott A, Andrew H, Scott N (2002) Next-product- to-buy models for cross-selling applications. J Interact Market 16 (3):59–75
Kumar V, Werner R (2006) Customer relationship management: A databased approach. John Wiley, New York
Kumar V (2006a) CLV: a path to higher profitability. Working Paper, University of Connecticut, Storrs
Kumar V (2006b) Customer lifetime value. In: Rajiv G, Marco V (eds) Handbook of Marketing Research. Thousand Oaks, Sage, CA, pp 602–627
Kumar V (2006c) Linking CLV to shareholders' value. Working Paper, University of Connecticut, Storrs
Kumar V, Luo M (2006) Linking an individual's brand value to the customer lifetime value: an integrated framework. Working Paper, University of Connecticut, Storrs
Levinthal, Daniel A, Mark F (1988) Dynamics of interorganizational attachments: auditor-client relationship. Adm Sci Quart 33:345–346
Lewis M (2003) Customer acquisition promotions and customer asset value. Working Paper, University of Florida, Gainseville
Lewis M (2005a) A dynamic programming approach to customer relationship pricing. J Manage Sci 51 (6):986–994
Lewis M (2005b) Incorporating strategic consumer behavior into customer valuation. J Market 69 (4):230–251
Li S, Sun B, Ronald W (2005) Cross-selling sequentially ordered products: an application to consumer banking services. J Market Res 42 (2):233–239
Pfeifer P, Robert C (2000) Modeling customer relationships as markov chains. J Interact Mark 14 (2):43–55
Reinartz W, Kumar V (2000) On the profitability of long-life customers in a noncontractual setting: an empirical investigation and implications for marketing. J Market 64(4):17–35
Reinartz W, Kumar V (2002) The mismanagement of customer loyalty. Harvard Bus Rev 80 (7):86–95
Reinartz VK, Thomas JS, Kumar V (2005) Balancing acquisition and retention resources to maximize customer profitability. J Market 69(1):63–79
Rust RT, Lemon KN, Zeithaml VA (2004) Return on marketing: using customer equity to focus marketing strategy. J Market 68(1):109–127
Schmittlein D, Morrison DG, Colombo R (1987) Counting your customers: who are they and what will they do next? Manage Sci 33:1–24

Tang LL, Thomas LC, Thomas S, Bozzetto J (2005) It's the economy stupid: comparison of proportional hazards models with economic and socio-demographic variables for estimating the purchase of financial products

Thomas J (2001) A methodology for linking customer acquisition to customer retention. J Mark Res 38(2):262–268

Thomas J, Reinartz W, Kumar V (2004a) Getting the most out of all your customers. Harvard Bus Rev 82(7/8):116–123

Thomas JS, Blattberg RC, Fox EJ (2004b) Recapturing lost customers. J Mark Res 41(1):31–45

Venkatesan R, Kumar V (2004) A customer lifetime value framework for customer selection and resource allocation strategy. J Market 68(4):106–125

Verhoef PC, Franses PH, Hoekstra JC (2001) The impact of satisfaction and payment equity on cross-buying: a dynamic model for a multi-service provider. J Retail 77(3):359–378